LETTERS FROM HOME

VOL. III

received thru

Tuieta

published by

Portals of Light, Inc.

1993

Letters From Home: Vol. III

Copyright © 1993 by Portals of Light, Inc.

ISBN 0-943365-17-1

Published by
Portals of Light, Inc.
P.O.Box 15621
Fort Wayne, IN 46885

Printed in the United States of America

FOREWORD

Over a period of several years the beloved ones of the Space Command have shared many messages and responded to many questions. <u>Letters From Home Vol. I</u> includes messages received 1982 through 1984. These are grouped as: Observations of our present state; concern and possible intervention; Earth man must alter his route; preparation for today, tomorrow and the new day; reunion preparation and reunion.

In <u>Letters From Home Vol. II</u> we "selected" a representation of messages received since 1984 regarding life on other planets; life on the ships; the seeding of planet Earth; their communication with us, and a simulated trip aboard a ship where the beloved ones responded to many of Earth mans questions.

This present volume and "Vol. IV" deal with the Space Commands comments regarding this earth, its occupants and institutions; the foreseen effects on the planet and people of the various energy infusions that are taking place; lift-off; the New Day.

Future volumes will include such things as extensive teachings they have shared that will help us to, learn - understand - KNOW.

In this volume, with the assistance of beloved Sarna, we have added certain introductory headings/comments/questions in order to help in the flow of material. Also we have "edited" certain portions of some of the messages. However, the channeled material that is included is exactly as received and there has been no attempt to alter the thought or feeling intent that was sent forth.

I, Tuieta, am greatly honored to be the means by which these thoughts can be shared with my fellow travelers on planet Earth. The channeled messages came as words/thoughts that were impressed upon my conscious mind by the beloved ones who are among our many unseen brothers, sisters, teachers, guides, friends. I make no claim regarding this material except to say I was used as an instrument that this TRUTH might be shared with mankind.

Please keep in mind the degree of purity of these messages is dependent upon the level of evolvement of myself, as the channel, at the time they were received.

As you read of these books may you be filled with the love, the joy, the peace, the brotherhood that I felt from the beloved ones as each message was shared through me, and may you glean from them that which will assist you in your preparation for the Day of the Golden Son.

Tuieta and David

CONTENTS

TITLE   **PAGE**

INTRODUCTION   1

INFUSION AND SUBSEQUENT ACTIVATION   3
 Expect the unexpected
 "Fall from grace"
 New state of consciousness
 Rays

PLANET EARTH   16
 Nebulae attached to earth galaxy
 Before man was
 Divine Thot
 "Let there be light"
 Moving cloud of energy
 Meteors coming to planet
 Fire in the sky
 Axis shifts
 Weather patterns
 Nuclear weapons and waste
 Ozone layer
 Helping the environment
 Time capsules
 Pyramids of Giza
 Stonehenge
 Ley lines
 Places: -- U.S.A., Canada, England
 -- Australia, New Zealand, Thailand
 Use of needles to heal Earth

Three days of darkness
Inner Earth

ADULT HU-MAN 78
Maintaining human form
Balance in the work setting
AIDS
Drugs and alcohol
Organ transplants
Premature death
The subconscious
Sleep and dreams
Ego
Emotions
Relationships
AIDS and homosexuality

CHILDREN 120
Desire peace for your children
Parents love
Mother-to-be
Expanding their visions
Devic children
Effect of Dark Brotherhood

ANIMAL KINGDOM 136
Their souls
Whales and dolphins

REACHING OUR FULL POTENTIAL 144
Teleportation and Levitation
Ascension
Work we came to do
Seeking quietness

Searching within
Our will and Divine Will
Law of Attraction

HELPING OTHERS 167
The dry sponge
Begin where the student is
Those who are suffering
Karma
Purpose of gatherings

TOOLS 183
Crystals
Crystal skulls
Music
Potions
Herbs
Algae
Inter-dimensional communications
Violet flame
Decrees
Exploring past lives
Shortcuts

INTRODUCTION

Greetings in the Light of the Radiant One. I am Sarna. Allow me to introduce myself. I am what could be referred to as Tuieta's cosmic baby sitter. My primary assignment is to assure that this "channel" or range of frequencies for this one is clear and ready at all times. I monitor her activities as well as that which is the activity of the Cosmos, noting how they interrelate one with another. For an example, if this one, Tuieta, has had a difficult day and her energy level is lagging, then I would notify those of the Command who would communicate with her, of that fact. They could then determine if it were necessary for a particular communique or if it might wait until she had had an opportunity to rest and recharge.

I am from the Second Galaxy. I came as a volunteer to planet Earth during this period of transition. Even as I assist, so it is I learn and grow in my own process. This growth is noted and assimilated by others of my galaxy who too have opportunity to share in the experience.

When last we put together a small volume, we shared with the reader a trip to a mother ship by way of a smaller vessel. You were given a tour of the ship, including thoughts shared concerning other planets and places. It was our intent to let you, the reader understand, though we operate in a different dimension, we too have "real form and real activities".

The hour has come when we have compiled another volume. This one has a different purpose. It is to let you on Earth know how we view your activities and the relationship of these activities to the Earth Mother. We want to speak to you of the changes which have already happened and which will happen in your upcoming years. How best can this be

1

presented without you the reader getting bored and feeling we are speaking about a place different than planet Earth?

We have decided to ask you to imagine a large crystalline town hall which has descended into your area. This town hall will allow entry only to those who desire in Truth, those who walk the Pathe of Light. It will be a place in which ones of Earth and ones of the Command can mingle and share. It will be a place where we can come at designated times to share thoughts and ideas.

Let us prepare for our first meeting. The town hall is securely in place. Ones of the Fleet have descended into a form which is compatible with your own. The topic for this meeting is energy infusion and the resultant activations. Your speakers will be Cuptan Fetogia, Lord Dionus, Commanders Beatrix and Monka, Captain Keilta, and myself. Let us begin.

INFUSION AND SUBSEQUENT ACTIVATION

Salutations, ones of planet Earth. I am Cuptan Fetogia speaking... [I reside on] the command ship of the Third Galaxy. I bring greetings from all ones of the Galaxy and from the Inner Council Ring. I have come to enter into the activation planning with the one that is known to you as the Lord Sananda. I come as the representative to offer counsel and assistance and to share of the knowing that has been afforded me. I come to enter into the ethers of the place that is known to you as the planet Earth, the Emerauld. It is the desire of the ones of Wisdom that I come to offer to the Blessed One their wisdom.

The ages of unknowing have been the lot of the ones that walk the face of the Earth Mother. The ages of darkness have been as that which is the accepted in the thought process of the children of the Earth Mother. This is being lifted from them. This is being removed to allow for a conscious understanding, yea knowing, on the part of all ones that are desirous to know. The hour of looking to the distant day is over. It is finis (finished). The call is for action now of all ones upon the planet.

Can you, Earth mans kind, not recognize the imminence of the approach? Look not to the morrow to begin to accept your responsibility and assume your accountability for that which is your own thoughts and actions. Look not to the grand of the distant day. Begin your actions NOW.

It is recognized by the Council of the ignorance of the masses of the ones that are with the Earth Mother. It is recognized that this shall require specific action on the part of the sons and daughters of the cosmic realm.

At the point in the cycle that is the solstice (December,1988) there shall be a great inpouring of cosmic and angelic energies directly from that which is known to you as the Godhead. This will bring about a great stirring within the individuals that dwell with the planet Earth. It is anticipated that most ones upon the planet shall react to this inpouring. Ones of Light, the faithful workers, shall be as ones to experience a heightened awareness and dimensional shift. It is for this that many have been prepared.

Expect the unexpected. Attune to the frequencies that are not of the accustomed vibrational level of your dimension. Accept the acceleration of your vibrational pattern. DO NOT FIGHT IT. This would result in a great unbalance for you. Indeed, it could be quite detrimental to your health mode.

It is anticipated by the ones of the Council that this inpouring shall bring about a great unbalance upon the planet. It is further anticipated that many of the un-enlightened ones shall react with a vibrational frequency that is as an onslaught to the ones of Light.

Do not, I repeat, do not engage yourselves in actions or activities that would bring great knowledge of your presence. Allow yourselves to be with like kind engaging in activities that would nurture and comfort you. Allow for your beings, all of your beings, to adjust to this alteration in vibrational frequency.

I have come as a volunteer representative of the Inner Council Ring to offer our humble assistance to the ones of the Fleet who serve of this sector. I shall remain in close communication with the ones of the Inner Council to allow for the shared wisdom and experience to be available for the ones of the Fleet.

This is a point in the cycle of events for the planet known as Earth which is a most critical one. It is a time in the evolution of the Earth mans kind peoples to recognize of their divinity, their purpose. Those that would choose the route of materialism and ego satisfaction are as ones that shall return to the dust. Their riches shall join with them as dust, allowing them to know that which they have worshipped is as naught, as is the false god.

Ye ones who would walk the Pathe of Light shall be as ones to recognize of these changes, both internally and externally. Allow for the experience. Silence the tongue that the totality might have opportunity to experience. Be as one content in the moment, allowing naught to dislodge you from your place.

We have watched of the actions of the ones of the Fleet and of the ones embodied on the planet. We know of the caring, the love, the tirelessness with which each serves. I am come to alert all ones to the Ones of all ones of creation, of the Cosmos. I am sent to bring to the ones of the Fleet the infusion of the energy patterns represented by the Inner Council Ring. I am sent to bring to all ones of all dimensions the awareness that none is alone, but is one cell in the totality that is known as Cosmic Man. I am sent to infuse into the ethers of the planet Earth the cosmic vibration to activate the alerted response by all the workers of the Light.

I am Cuptan Fetogia. I [reside at this hour on] the Command ship of the Third Galaxy as it enters the ethers of the planet that is known as Earth. I bring greetings from the Elohim, the Inner Heart of the Divine One.

CUPTAN FETOGIA (continues) ...I spoke to you of the intro-duction of a combination of vibrational patterns of energies that have been introduced during that particular time. This vibrational pattern of energies shall be experienced by you upon the planet as an increase in intensity, allowing you to in-tegrate that which you are in your individual totalities. There are ones stationed about your planet that are closely monitor-ing you and your reception mode to these frequency patterns.

It has been judged from the Council of the Central

Source that you within your sun system, particularly your planet, cannot accept or tolerate a compatible vibration with these energies unless they are divided into fractional introduction periods. Hence, many of you will experience your full moon as a period of heightened activity. And those periods that are known to you as your eclipses shall also be ones of increased intensity.

As you allow the infusion of these vibrational frequencies and begin to adjust to them in a compatible mode, many ones about the planet who have chosen to remain uninformed, hence un-enlightened, are ones that shall experience these in a mode of agitation... Do not, I emphasize, <u>do not</u> get caught up in the sweeping tide of reaction, but allow for the flow with the energy adjustment. Recognize, inhabitants of planet Earth, you have entered into an acceleration mode. Allow yourselves the opportunities to adjust to this.

We shall continue to observe you, to offer our counsel for your consideration to help you through this initial period. Those of you that have entered into a hurried schedule, I would strongly urge you to evaluate its necessity. Each of you need your periods of solitude, of quietness, to allow for your own integration, as well as assisting the Earth Mother in this process. Be advised of additional numbers of the Fleet have entered to assist you during this particular period.

You recognize the whole pattern for your planet is, indeed, a tenuous hold on your present system. We are endeavoring to assist you in this transition, so that you might have the least amount of upheaval...

BEATRIX Blessings in the Light of the Radiant One to you... For those of you that are not familiar with my energy pattern, I am of the universal university on Helox. I speak particularly to those ones that are engineers, that are builders, that are thought processors, those ones that would bring in to manifestation the thought that has been given to them. Many ones, many graduates of the university are now upon your planet. As I would speak, I would desire a stirring within these ones that they would begin to remember, that they would recall some of the teachings, some of the lessons that have been shared with them as they would sit at the knee of their teacher...

We are coming into a period of great, and I repeat great, unbalance for ye ones of Earth. It shall be a period when all that is within you will be heightened and magnified. It is a period that can either bring about great Light within you, or it can bring about increased negativity or the darker forces. Man has choice, and it is up to his choice how this period shall be for him. It is a time that many ones of the Light shall be tested to their very limit they feel, but it will not be to their limit, for they shall be given the strength to come up and over that which has tested them.

It is a time that shall also bring forth great good and peace, if that is the path that man shall choose. It is up to his choice and how he would react to that which is sent to him. This is part of the new alignment of the planets as Earth is prepared for her initiation.

Do not be confused that this is the initiation for Mother Earth to go into the next dimension but rather it is an initiation for her to rid herself of certain belts of energy that have girded her, and allow herself to be girded with the new Light belts that are being set up around her. It is also an opportunity for her to further align herself with the positive energies of her sister planets, particularly the planets of love and harmony. It is a time that she shall leave of the binding energies that have held her in this present frame of this age and allow her to come into a greater balance with Venus and Saturn.

This is the initiation that Mother Earth shall prepare for. Then as the energies from this planet shall mingle with the energies from the stronger positive ones she shall gain in her overall cleansing. She shall gain in strength to cast off that which has been so long bound in her ethers.

Yes, my dear [ones], it is an initiation for Earth, and it

shall also be an initiation for each of you that are with her. Do not be surprised at anything that happens for the most unexpected is likely to occur.

For our ones of Light it is a testing of your balance and at-one-ment with the Light and the Light Forces. It is a period that can be a great awakening or it can be a period of calamity, all according to how you choose to use that which is given to you. But isn't that the truth for man of Earth even in this day? He has his choice how he would use that which is given to him. He has his choice how he will react to that which is freely shared with him. It shall be a most glorious day throughout all eternity when he can see the obvious choice, and he can take his steps with us along the Universal Path...

Can you tell us more about specific dates for the energy shifts?

MONKA I am Monka to reply to your question. I greet you in the Light of the Source, that which each is for ever more.

Let us address this thing which you call dates, times... [There is an ongoing infusion of energy which is coming forth in drops or waves] and each one responds to a specific vibration or a specific wave. And there will be one -- that which is called a channel -- that will respond to this vibration so they will say there is going to be something that happens in a specific span of time. And this is true. For those souls who respond to that drop or that portion of the wave it will be a very intense time for them. There will be others that will go through that wave and they will have no experience...

I would offer your consideration to see what you are responding too, and listen and feel and experience what you are responding too. And know that you can follow this pattern... Mark this on your calendar; then see on your calendar when is the next time that you have this feeling -- you go through a similar experience. It will not be identical, but it will

8

be similar. See what the wave pattern is that you respond to. And then when ones would say to you such and such will happen on such and such a day, you will know that they speak of a vibration that is not a vibration that you are tuned with or it is a vibration that you are very muchly attuned with. But you cannot forecast that this will happen on this day, at this hour because there is a variable which is called man. And there is a variable which is called the collective consciousness. And this has impact upon the vibrations as they are experienced upon the planet.

And I am most grateful that you allowed me to share this. For indeed there is nothing that is wrong, if you will, for one to say that there will be an energy infusion on such a such a period, for indeed there is a group of entities, a group of souls that will respond to that energy, but there will also be another group that will not. And so you must see what your pattern is. What do you respond to? And then you know when you should take your vacations.

MONKA (continues) ...Man, since his creation from the Divine Breath has been on a journey to evolve into his birthright. In order for him to do this there must be certain sustaining energies that are shared with him. Here I must hesitate for the energies are always there. It is that man is not to a level of awareness that he can appreciate them. He is not of a vibratory frequency to be aware of them. All of creation is on a cyclic journey of evolution. All of creation is on a journey to reach that which is the Divine Essence that is their creation.

Man has asked the question of, "Why?". If man were perfect at his creation then why must he experience evolution to again be perfect? You of Earth have used of the term, "fall from grace". You have gone forth from the Creator Source, and if you choose to use the term "fallen" then that is your choice. Man has not fallen but has embarked on a great and a wondrous journey. This seed that was his beginning was quite small in its creation. It cannot be seen by your micro-scopes. It cannot be measured on one of your scales. As it goes forth it gathers in its richness in creation. It gathers in its fullness of evolution. It is a process that allows the seed to become the creator as well as the creation.

Please if you will, keep in mind that statement -- to become the creator as well as the creation. The seed is ini-tially as your small infant for it cannot care for itself and must be sustained by others for a brief period. It is watched over and nurtured by those that have evolved in their own creator-creation state. Hence it is creation that has come forth to begin its journey to the realization that it is creator. Only then can this seed return to the Divine Principle and be as one with It. This is the evolution of all ones that have come forth. This is the state that all of us are in. This is the journey that all of us are experiencing...

KEILTA Greetings in the Light of the Radiant One. Keilta here. With your permission, I shall continue the discourse that our brother Monka had started at an earlier time.

Energy. Energy released to Earth. This would lead one to assume that the energy that is introduced to Earth at a specific time is a new and different form of energy than had been earlier available to Earth man, yet our brother has stated that all energy is available to all ones. There seems to be a bit of a contradiction here. Yet, there is not. On the dimensions that are above the ones that are enjoyed by ear-theans at this time, all energy is available to all ones according to their ability to receive them and to utilize them to the highest good. This is a known fact for all of us.

However, and here is the difference between your dimension and ours, there is a curtain that filters what is available to Earth man -- a curtain that is ever changing and vibrating. This allows that man on Earth cannot receive that which would not be utilized for the highest good of all ones on the planet as well as those of us that dwell beyond. Think of

10

this curtain as a membrane that constantly monitors what is allowed within its interior such as the membrane of your cellular systems. As the substance within the membrane is ready to receive nutrients from the outside the membrane allows for the nutrients to pass through to feed the inner bodies of the cell. This is also an accurate description of the membrane that is around Earth. This is a protective substance for those that are with Earth as well as those that are beyond her, just as the membrane of the cell acts as a buffer between the inner cell and the outer space.

So to resume. The ones of Earth have asked to be fed, to receive the nutrients from beyond the membrane. The membrane thus allows the nutrients or energy to pass through to feed the ones on the planet. So in truth, energies are released to Earth as ones of Earth as well as Earth herself are ready to receive. There is actually no separation, only a state of balance. Nothing can be received until such time as there is a need for that which would be given.

You of the planet have achieved a specific point in your evolutionary cycle that you are ready to allow more of the Christed energies to be released into the planet and its ethers. It is to say that the majority of the ones on the planet are ready to receive. This is not to give the impression that all ones on the planet have achieved the same vibratory acceptance, but that the majority have. It is also recognized that as the energies are allowed to penetrate the membrane that the ones that are not ready for this alteration in vibratory status will not react in the same manner as the ones that are ready. Indeed, if you will observe your pattern of past introduction of specific energies, you will note that ones on the planet have felt a need to take the lives of others, the need to rob and the need to dominate. Theirs has been a reaction to the energies.

Those that are ready to receive the change in the energy patterns, feel a change in their overall vibratory rate. They act with and in accordance with the energies that are with them. There is the difference, dear brothers and sisters.

DIONUS ...My beloved ones of Earth, though you may feel that you know me not, I assure you I know each of you. I have come as the representative to sit upon the council, and offer that portion of wisdom that I have on behalf of all of you.

As you are aware there is a great interest in your planet and its evolution. Many ones from throughout the galaxies have come to your planet to experience specific portions of your evolution, to observe you, to work with you, to try to learn, to understand you, that which you are.

Of a long distant day there were many planets about the universes that were in a similar state of evolution that you are now in. And indeed, they have evolved past that stage. For many ones this was a long, long time ago, and they have forgotten.

And so it is now that ones come and they look to you. And as they do they see their own history, they see their own evolution. They also recognize that their evolution is tied to yours, just as you are tied to them. And they cannot evolve, they cannot grow along their paths, until you have had the opportunity to evolve on yours.

Your scientists on Earth have put forth great theories according to your Earth's origin, according to what will happen, and what possibly can happen. In other instances, they are looking through things with a most myopic view. You, the inhabitants of Earth are rolling into a new berth, to enter into a new state of awareness, a new state of consciousness, a decided change in vibratory rate. Those that feel their energies are not compatible with this change shall be removed to a place that is of a more compatible nature.

As we gather about on behalf of all of planet Earth, we do so with the purpose of assisting you, that would raise your vibratory rate, and to give to you the tools, the preparation, the wherewith to enter into a new state of consciousness -- and indeed, in future days to enter into a state which is a vibratory rate much greater than that one which you now experience.

The Lords of the Hierarchy have decreed that specific energy patterns shall come to Earth. There are ones that will call these "rays". There are ones that will call this by many names. The name is of no consequence. It is what you do with the energy that comes to you, and how you would choose to grow along your path.

You of Earth have a lean towards being quite busy, busy in physical activities. And you are as the ostrich, for you would hide your head at the thought of sitting in quietness and contemplation. Your greatest growth and your greatest evolvement, your greatest accomplishments are made in those periods when you sit in quiet contemplation. This is a truth that your brothers and sisters of your universe and of the Cosmos have learned. This is a truth which you try so desperately to escape.

May I suggest to you that you spend more time in meditation, in quiet contemplation, that you might truly learn of the greater truths, that you might feel as your vibratory rate is accelerated, and you grow in your attunement -- much as a string on one of your string instruments is tightened ever so slightly that it might reach its perfect pitch.

This is a most exciting time for you of Earth, for you ones that have volunteered to be with Earth. And just as quietly you feel the joy within your heart, we too feel the joy within our hearts in anticipation of the reunion of the families that shall come together, of friendships, of loved ones that shall be reunited.

You Light Workers, the legion of volunteers, are indeed a carefully selected group that has entered embodiment on planet Earth. We are humbled to serve with you. And as I have come to join with the rest of the command under the guidance of the beloved Ashtar, may I offer to you my assistance, my support and my love. Thank you dear ones. I shall stand ever ready to offer my assistance to you.

The term "rays" was mentioned. Could you elaborate further?

SARNA ...The rays come to your planet -- and as you would call them rays, perhaps, I would better interpret them as vibrational frequencies or patterns that are shared with ones upon planet Earth -- these vibrational frequencies or patterns hold specific concepts for Earth mankind. That which you would call the ray of the first ray, the second ray, the third and fourth, and so on till you have gone through the seven rays -- and you will eventually acknowledge that there are twelve rays -- are being experienced by Earth mankind in a polarity way.

We will take that which is the First Ray, the one of Will, of Power. You will note as you would look about your planet how this ray is being used in its polarities. Is this not so? So it is also with the other rays or vibrational frequencies that are being shared with the ones who are in embodiment on planet Earth. All come at the same intensity to the planet; however, at specific portions or specific places within the cycle of the evolution of all of ones upon the planet, there are those that are more predominant than there are others. It is according to the evolution or the acceptance of the conscious level of acceptance of Earth mankind.

You will note that man is having difficulty with that which would be considered loving one another. This particular concept has been with him for a period or a cycle, and yet, it is not one that is easily accepted. And man uses that which you would call the negative polarity of even that ray.

Man has opportunity to use all rays within balance. However, it is not his choice at this hour to accept them or to use them in their balanced state, but rather, man is experiencing the polarities. It is only as man will come within a balance within himself that he will be able to experience the rays in their balanced state, for the degree of acceptance is in direct proportion to the degree of acceptance of the divinity that is within each...

I would add a thought that there is that which is called the Eighth Ray that is coming forth. And ones would say this is the ray of the New Age, or the new thinking process. This comes in its infancy, if you would desire to use that term, and it again is being experienced in its polarity, and the balance is of a minimum at this point.

Could you tell to us more about the Eighth Ray energies?

SARNA ...Those of you that are familiar with your numerological studies know that the number eight is a balancing one between the higher attunement and that which you are now experiencing. This ray, this energy pattern, perhaps would be a more accurate way of phrasing it, is one that assists specific ones in specific ways, as well as allowing the general populous to grow in their own awareness and attunement with the higher dimensions. Ones of the Pleiadean connection shall find a great familiarity with this energy pattern, for indeed, this has been used, has been utilized within this group of stars for several hundred years. It is being introduced, or it has come to Earth to assist you in your own evolvement as well as the evolvement in toto of Earth mankind.

I would add a word, a thought here. And that one is, that just as there are ones that find this energy pattern most compatible and most elevating, it also has the reverse effects upon others. As in all instances, there are reactions of a polarity nature upon your planet.

* * * * *

Our meeting has concluded. May you now return to your dwelling place even as we return to ours. Peace be with you until we come together once more.

Sarna out.

15

PLANET EARTH

Good evening ladies and gentlemen, co-workers of Light. I am glad to see so many of you return after our first meeting. I trust this past period has been a pleasant one for you. Tonight as we gather we shall hear shared thoughts concerning the effect of cosmic activity on planet Earth and her inhabitants. Remember nothing happens or is experienced in the singular. Our speakers will be Cuptan Fetogia, Lord Dionus, Commanders Ashtar, Soltec, Monka, Hatonn, Jokhym, Beatrix, Captain Keilta and myself.

* * * * *

Greetings, brothers and sisters of planet Earth. I am that one who is known as Soltec to most of you. I might be considered in your terms as that which is a geophysicist, for indeed, my primary responsibility, as you are aware, is to observe, anticipate, record and evaluate the geophysical changes which are going on upon your planet, now and at the later periods also...

The galaxy which holds the sun system of Earth's place has entered into a most turbulent space in the Cosmos. As you are aware the galactic systems are not stagnant but rather are constantly moving in a pre-ordained path. Each is given its orbit within the grand orbit of the central sun. Because of unusual cosmic activity the galactic system has entered an area of increased turbulence and bombardment. The result will be an increase in the activities of the galaxy as well as the planetary sun systems.

The sun of your system will send forth additional flares as it experiences the bombardment of its surrounding galaxy. This will bring about unbalance for the planets within its system. The earth planet and its inhabitants will experience the results of the solar flares. There will be increased and intense geo-physical activity. Precipitation patterns will alter greatly. There will also be an increase in the amount of radioactive materials in the air about the planet. Do not, I repeat, do not engage in sunning yourselves at this period. Increase in the radonic, alpha, zroc and other rays of lesser magnitude are to be experienced.

The individual upon the planet will experience physical and emotional unbalance in direct proportion to the unbalance of the planet. Diet, rest and moderate exercise are to be given prime consideration. Increase the amount of fluids in-taken. Provide for yourselves ample space for quietness and meditation. Let the communication frequency be open for direction and guidance.

We are placing a belt of ships about the planet Earth from north to south pole and south to north pole just as we have them about the equator. Larger ships have been secured at strategic points to assist in balancing. The bombardment experience by Earth can cause an increase in the erratic orbital pattern she is already experiencing.

Feel of yourselves in a giant storm in which you are being bombarded by particums too small to be observed, but large enough to cause sensation. Such is the situation now.

SOLTEC (continues) ...Let me briefly explain what has happened and what the earth is and will be experiencing as a result of the experience. Within the orbital structure for the galaxy housing planet Earth and its sun system there is a collection of other sun systems. These combine with various star patterns to make up the galaxy which is known to you as the home and origin of Earth. The origin of this galaxy and all other galaxies began as nebulae about the Great Central Sun. This, because of its place has been seen as the origin of life or movement as it is known. These nebulae have consolidated, divided, and consolidated ad infinitum since the moment of the original.

According to cyclic patterns the galaxies do not come into a collision course with one another, but rather exist in a harmonious manner. Travel between galactic systems is easily accomplished because of this. However, as the formation of a new nebulae is in process, all galaxies are touched by that formation to add to it. This was anticipated for you within this your calender year (1992). This brief fusion and infusion was the primary reason for the projected geophysical changes of this calender year. The initial fusion has happened. The new nebulae has attached itself to your galaxy.

Because of the intensity of the action within the nebulae, the plus and minus charges within the galactic system have begun to move about in an intense manner. Volcanoes throughout the galaxy are erupting, spewing forth large amounts of matter. Cloud coverage about many of the planets have been severely disrupted. Intense waters are spilling to surfaces which have been quite dry. The intensity of the very basis of the galaxy, its base part, is causing great change for all within the galaxy.

You who are on planet Earth, sit within the galaxy sufficiently that the ripple effect of the fusion should not be as intense as it would be if you were on its outer fringes. Ships have been dispatched to all planets of your sun system to assist in their stabilization. Other civilizations have taken their own protective actions. You upon your planet, because of your desire to maintain as the "center of your universe", have not been so advised. We have taken the action necessary for your safety and protection.

We urge you to recognize that all about you and all that is you -- except your divinity -- is of the basic material of your galaxy. Recognize that at the very elementary level the particums of your own creation are reacting to the introduction to this nebulae infusion. As you know of this so it is that you can prepare for the resulting imbalance within you. You can also be alerted to the potential unbalance of your planet. You may then take the steps necessary to assure your own well being and safety. This is not, I repeat, this is not an energy infusion for you or the planet, but is a reaction to the infusion and attachment of the nebulae...

...This particular nebulae attached itself to your galaxy approximately two-hundred earth years ago. However, its impact has not been experienced by your place in the galactic system until this which is your calendar year. This intensity of vibration which I shall discuss will continue through the first half of your calendar year, and then there will be a somewhat of a leveling period as far as the nebulas is concerned.

The intensity of vibration, or alteration in pattern which you have experienced is the result of the initial vacuum, if you will, created in the center of the nebulas which attracts to it from the parent or supporting galaxy. Once that has been filled, shall we say in your literal terms, then there is more of a flowing or an exchange which takes place with the nebulae and the supporting system.

There will be those who would question my use of the term "nebulae" instead of "nebulas." In this instance, either term is correct, for the nebulas for the new galactic formation consists of multiple nebulae, each one its own unique totality. Shall we say, each nebulas contains many facets, each a complete nebulae, or nebulas, within itself. So as I would use the terms interchangeably, it is because of the cosmic makeup of this nebulas.

As I stated earlier, there is the impact which is felt by the supporting galaxy, even to its depth of center point. This can affect the electromagnetic field of your planet and will have impact on navigational systems who still use these methods of navigation. We see it merely as a swaying of ley lines and navigational routes and patterns, knowing they will come into stabilization. We can travel upon them prior to their stabilization; however, our journeys are indeed not as smooth or as expedient as they would be.

See this attachment to your galaxy as the infant within the womb. It is being fed, it is being nourished, it is forming because of the energies which are shared with it by the supporting galaxy or, at this point if you will, its mother. When it has received all which it can receive from this particular formation, it will propel itself, with the assistance of your galaxy into the Cosmos to then attach itself to another galaxy. We would expect in the next five million earth years its formation, solidification, and habitation would be complete.

When you would give this careful consideration, there would be a certain amount of joy to this experience and the knowledge of this experience to know by thought, you, as individuals and as collective have shared with and been involved in, the creation of a new galactic system. What have you shared with it? What have you contributed to its formation? And indeed, what have you gained from the whole experience? This opens a multiplicity of avenues, does it not?...

At this point, Earth has been stabilized through the experience and we are merely waiting for the initiation of the flow rather than the pull of the vacuum or, shall we say, the push to fill the vacuum.

MONKA Greetings beloveds. ...I share thoughts to clarify and perhaps expand the understanding you might have of the activities of your cosmos, of that which is your sun system.

Before you were, there was that which caused movement, with the result of your universe. Is this not so? Ones upon your plane seem to separate their scientific knowledge and their spiritual knowledge, or the understanding of either one. There appears to be difficulty in accepting the fact the Source -- that which you call God -- and that which is the understanding within your science of the stars, of the atoms and such, are interrelated and interwoven.

Oft times this one through which I speak has said, "God does not do things in a hurry. But rather, God is methodical. It is only man who does not see the pattern."

We smile when she says this, for there is a great accuracy in this statement. Man does not see the pattern. So when there is a chain of events which comes into play, he sees it as a catastrophe or as a phenomenon, and he wonders at the miracles of the Source, and how this can be done. Such an attitude is indicative of a limited understanding, for to understand the workings of all that is about you is to understand the workings of that which is the universe, the Cosmos -- that which rests within the hand of the Divine One.

Light is quite often referred to by ones of this Age of Newness. Yet, do they understand what Light is? What is it they say? What is it they truly are saying?

First, from the Source, within your level of experience, came forth the thought. And as the thought went forth there was Light. In your Holy Book was this not the first creation of the Source? "Let there be Light." What does this Light? What is it? Light is brought about by friction. It is either the intense coming together or the intense coming apart. It is indicative of a change in pattern from the original. It means there is movement, and that which was in a state of inertia is now in a state of ertia.

Light is indicative of change -- at one moment and at all moments thereafter. When you call forth the Light and you surround yourselves in Light, you are saying "I desire change for my highest good, and I ask that the Divine assist the divine within me in bringing forth all of the energies to bring about that change for my highest good." To wear a protection of Light is to say you have -- and I speak of the divinity within you -- you have arranged the activity of your electromagnetic field which you are, into a pattern which cannot be penetrated. It is a pattern which is constantly moving and which repels that which is not of the same vibration and at-one-ment as the exterior wall or membrane of your electromagnetic field, your energy field, if you will.

And perhaps I should re-trace my steps and say to you, we must acknowledge all of creation is energy or the potential of being energy. Energy is constantly moving -- it is taking in, it is releasing. It is constantly in a state of ertia. Oft times, in your language of words, you say "energy" and "Light" as being synonymous. It is not quite accurate, but for most of you, you understand what you are saying. However, there are those of you who have placed a higher esteem on Light than you have on energy. You see Light as the divine expression of energy. And as you review through the various causal planes, Light indeed is the closest to that which you know as the Creator's.

But let us look at that which is the action. One who was and is closely attached to Earth, who is master and chohan of the fourth ray (Serapis Bey), has given teachings of particums. And he has spoken of the electrom and the protom, but he has spoken primarily of particums. Particums can be understood as that which is activated by the Divine Thot (Thought) to bring about the atomic structure, which can then be translated into planets, stars, moons, vegetation, animals, and those who carry the divine spark, which are truly those which are called Universal Man.

Particums are small units of energy which come together to form the basis of that which you know as Creation. They are units of measurement which are beyond the calibration of Earth mankind. From these particums you have your atoms of various elements. Are you following me?

Now these elements are created from the particums in one of two ways; actually, one of three ways: There is that first which is the impaction, which is the coming together with such an intensity it causes a spark, a friction, with resultant sparks of light. There is that which is the pulling away, or the division of a particum, an energy unit -- a breaking up of the energy unit which, too, causes a spark, i.e., light. The third is the rapid movement of particums as they seek ones of like kind to establish a pattern with resultant form. It is that movement as they pass one another which also produces a friction, i.e., resultant light. Can you begin to see why this is the first known, or understood, principle of the action or the expression of Deity within your level of understanding? Light. It was indicative of the entry of the Divine Thot.

Now once this began you can visualize the beauty which would be seen in that which has been the unexpressed void of Creation as myriads and myriads of sparks of divine activity, of activity of movement of energy awakens to move into forms, to move into the proper place, to give you upon your planet the correct composition for you to breathe, the water for you to drink, and the vegetation to sustain you. Is that not wondrous?

I spoke of three ways this light was brought forth. Your scientists now take light, which is energy; they take sound, which is energy; and as energy moves about and you have light or friction, you also have sound. The universal hum -- perhaps could this be its origin? I'll let you wrestle with that question.

But your scientists interpret light in that which is the energy they understand upon your planet. And they use various terms to identify or explain the quantity of energy they are measuring, or denoting. For instance, one way of denoting light is the measurement of photon activity. Another way, perhaps, would be to measure phonon activity. Each is indicative of measuring a small, very, very small microscopic measurement of energy movement which may produce itself with resultant light or sound. Do you understand that?

Now sound follows light. You must first have the action; then you have the light with the resultant sound. This is shown to you as you have your great storms about your planet, is it not? When you have the lightning that dances across your skies and you hear the rumblings, and they would sound as if they were coming from the very depths of the soul of the Creator, they could be so intense. But one follows the other. It would be dependent upon what you were measuring or observing, as to what word or what name you would give it. A "quantum" or a "quanta" is merely that which is so minute it is incomprehensible to the collective consciousness of Earth, the size or dimension of anything so small.

So there are ones who would receive lessons, and these lessons would have to do with the photon or phonon.

Within Creation you have that which has not come to its fullest expression. Some would call them places of great density. I would choose "intensity of activity." They are that which moves about cosmically and have effect upon all that which comes into their path. You see your sun system as being a relatively stationary thing. It is very difficult for you to visualize your sun is moving. And that which is in their orbital path about the sun -- your home and mine -- we are moving about the sun system. But the sun system is also moving within the galaxy. And the galaxy is moving within the level of expression of Source. If not, would we not have stagnation, and there would be no thing. You would not be and I would not be.

So there is movement. And if there is movement in all of that which is Creation, then is it not logical there are places in Creation which would seem to not be in the greatest harmony. This has been explained to you in conceptual terms before, but perhaps there are ones who need more specificity, hmm?

So you are coming into a cloud -- that which is a cloud of great activity. You will pass through this cloud, for it would be as it would sweep over your sun system. And if you will acknowledge space in time, then you would acknowledge the planets of your sun system would be in various places about your sun. And to have distance in space, then you would say there are some of your planets of your sun system, who may enter into this before the Sun enters into it, would you not? But if you do not acknowledge space or time, then it would be this would happen to all of your sun system instantaneously, would it not? That is not so difficult, is it? So you must look at that which you acknowledge.

When it was the beloved Cuptan, the Elder Statesman, brought forth those energies which are recorded in the "Conclaves", it was noted these energies were those which specifically had impact on the consciousness of man. If you recognize man is not an isolated entity but has impact upon the Earth Mother, upon the fauna and the flora as well, you then would know these energies have had impact upon these areas as well. But the route of impact has been more specialized, shall we say, than to say energies have been released.

These patterns which have been released have come as a cloak about planet Earth to intensify the consciousness of the individual which carries divinity within it; i.e., man -- Earth man.

Man has reacted, in most instances, with great intensity. You will note you have had that which have been several wars, confrontations with arms, by Earth mankind with Earth mankind since the introduction of this alteration in vibration. This is an example of a specific alteration in energies that is not cosmic.

Throughout your level from the Creator you have groups of particums which are seeking to establish; be it form, be it... It is that part of your dimension which has not yet been utilized in definition of its energy. It is a random, moving cloud of energy -- and you recognize clouds can be several millions long or wide. These move about your galaxy, other galaxies, all of Creation, until such point as they have reached a stabilized pattern, with the result of a definition of that which they are.

Let us say these clouds are energy particums who are seekers about the Cosmos, even as you are seekers, are you not? And when you first began to seek, were you not moving about in a most random fashion? Indeed, at times it was almost irrational, was it not? So it is these particums are doing the same.

There are these clouds about. Earth will experience this impact of one of these clouds. The impact shall be determined by that which is the collective of man upon the planet. If man is that which is balanced within his own energy field and in alignment, there will be minimal impact for him. For those who operate in great confusion and lack of focus, they shall feel a great intensity of lack of focus and confusion. Particums will be attracted to that which is similar to themselves.

Now, man -- that which is the universal expression of the Source -- carries within him, either acknowledged or unacknowledged, his own magnetic unit. This unit is aligned with that which is the magnetic field of the planet on which he resides. If man was not aligned with that field, then the magnetic field of the individual would be in such disarray there would be no individual. So there is an alignment between the magnetism of the planet and the magnetism of the deity within the individual, on any specified planet, regardless of what vibration they are in.

When you -- we -- for all of Creation is exposed to these clouds -- when you go through these, because there is such disharmony and there is such rushing about, such activity, the electromagnetic field of the planets, the suns, whatever system, is affected, and the electromagnetic field of the individual is also affected. This can be a very disheartening experience, or it can be a very uplifting one, both for man and the planet. It is according to the alignment of the individual in their own electromagnetic field as to how they shall react, or act, during this experience.

The planet will attract to it, or send away from it, according to the harmony or compatibility of the unexpressed particums. Some would see these as showers of light. And remember, I gave you three causes of light. Some would not, depending on their density level. All is moving; all is changing. That which would be called stagnation does not exist. Stagnation denotes that which has no movement, and all of Creation and all facets of Creator experiencing Creation, is in a state of movement.

Now there comes into play that which is called "focus" and "desire." As the beloved Cuptan has spoken -- and I would not be so presumptuous as to repeat what he has said, other than for a gentle reminder from me as to look at your focus. Is your focus to save your form, to preserve yourselves because you do not know what is beyond your moment? Or is your focus that which is divine -- to bring forth the greatest expression of the god within you of which you are capable in any experience, i.e., that which you call the experience of life on planet Earth? I cannot determine your focus. I have no desire to determine your focus. You -- only you -- can do this.

Fear brings about a state of inertia. Fear paralyzes the electromagnetic field of an individual and allows for no flow. If you could see in space an individual who is locked in fear, you would see a great hole in Creation, for there would be no movement, there would be no thing. Hence, they would not be. For it is only that which is energy which is vibrating, which is moving, that is defined as Creation. Do you understand what I am saying, my brethren? My desire for you is to release the fear which has been so inbred within you, so you might allow for the ertia of that which is life.

There is no thing which comes about which has not been put into cosmic play for the highest good of all ones. Can you not accept that? Light -- movement. Absence of movement -- that which you call darkness.

I have spoken of many aspects as we have come together at this point. I say to you to ponder them well. Ponder them well. My greatest desire for each of you is to go forth claiming your own divinity and allowing that which is the God within you -- the facet of the Original Source -- to come forth, to express itself in its fullest. Truly, then, will I be one with all which you are.

In Conclave: 3rd Meeting, it talks about meteors coming to planet Earth in 1995. Can this schedule be changed?

MONKA Oh, yes my child, it can be changed. It can be changed by you, Earth mankind, and the consciousness and the thought that you hold and maintain. But recognize even as I say this to you, it is up to the totality that is man and those ones that would seek to control and to manipulate the consciousness of man. This is the determining factor.

As we see that which are the events which are before you, we do not see any alteration in the anticipated plan. For indeed, man does not accept responsibility for himself. He quickly places his own power within the hands of others, shrugging his shoulders and giving "they" the responsibility for all that is about him. It is only when man again will collect his own power, take control of himself, and accept the responsibility for that which he is, an instrument of divinity, and walk in that path, that great changes can come about most expediently upon your planet. This is our desire. Within the Brotherhood of the Cosmos, this is our desire. However, this one that is called Earth mankind is rather obstinate in the plan of things. And so, at this point, we do not anticipate any changes from that which was given in the (3rd) Conclave.

SOLTEC ...I would smile at Earth mankind and his concern with these meteors. Indeed they are at this time known by your scientists. There is that which is called a Star Wars program. There has been the thought put forth that these instruments would be able to send forth beams to break up meteors that come within your ethers. Your scientists are aware of them as they approach. However, the velocity with which they travel is not one that is causing the alarm which could be within the scientific community. We stand, we have the capability to divert one, two, three, or all of these as we await instruction from the Commander-in-Chief. However, that diversion depends upon the collective consciousness of Earth mankind...

All is going according to schedule. And this which

you would call your decade of your 1990's promises for all of you to be a decade of much activity.

May I suggest to those of you who work closely with the Earth Mother to secure some sort of a map, a globe, or something on which you might trace the fault lines, so you may sit in your quietness focusing, balancing energies, healing if you will, in these areas. The Earth as it is receiving a bombardment is having a structurally difficult period and this would be of assistance for her...

We would also bring to your awareness the number of earthquakes which are going on about your planet. Some of you may even consider keeping a diary of this activity, this shaking, this vibration that is going on. Again, it shows that the Earth Mother is weary and she is breaking from one shell to another.

It is known to us there are those who have up to the minute information concerning the seismic activity about your planet. If you also would concentrate your thoughts in this way, you would help in the stabilization and the balancing.

The cosmic imbalances that are going on, for instance, the meteors, would this be what the prophets talked about when they mentioned the fire in the sky?

SOLTEC ...Indeed. They would appear, or were shown in ancient days upon your planet as "fiery chariots" which streaked across the sky. Now recognize even as we would speak of those which are the meteors, you have before this a shower in which smaller "chariots of fire" will be coming across your skies. You will note with this particular shower of the smaller ones, you will see a variety of colors, which in most instances you do not see but rather you would see that which would be the fiery, the gold, and the red that is mixed together. But you will begin to note as you see this display in your sky, you will see a variety of colors particularly a lot of green. And this is because of the electromagnetic reaction

29

with your pole and the magnetism of the pole altering the physical structure of these as they would enter the Earth, and the chemical, the element of which they have come from, shows up as a green glow.

Would you talk about the axis shifts?

SOLTEC ...As each of you is aware you are sitting in a precarious way upon your own axis, are you not? Because you are sitting at an angle. This has effect upon how your weather changes, your weather patterns, all of these things effect you upon your planet. As you go through your orbit around the star, which you call the sun, your planet has a minute particle bombardment and you literally move back and forth within a range, your axis does. If you could see yourselves, you would tilt. You are moving back and forth. You have accustomized to this shifting, to this slight deviation, shall we say. I believe in your measurements it would be something as slight as .003 degrees. So it would not seem great to you, but yet it does have impact upon you.

The axital shift, which has been discussed by many ones and through many ones will be the result of the meteors coming into direct contact with your planet. When you have boom, boom, boom, boom, you affect the axis because you have a great impact in one portion of your planet, which will then draw your planet in a particular way.

The axis shift which will come about will be more of a tilt. Some of you are feeling it will be as much as 90 degrees. Indeed it will not be that much. But it will be more of a tilt. And in essence you will say your North Pole has moved, and your South Pole has moved. And as this happens you will be entering a tilt from say straight perpendicular, as an illustration only, to perhaps 10, even up to 15 degrees. And as you come across this way it will have effect from a planetary point of view, on your weather systems, on your earth changes, on your uprising of various land masses. The movement of the land masses, the earthquakes will be brought about primarily by the explosion or the contact of the meteors as they would come to your planet.

The alteration in your axis, will bring about melting of the ice caps which are at either end, which will produce a rise in the water levels. And that which is high will not receive the same amount of waters as that which is the lower or the basin areas. However, with your tilt and your contact with your meteors, this will produce quakings which will alter the land arrangement, shall we say, of the land masses on your planet.

So you have not one aspect, but you have an effect of many aspects coming together. Even as you would look now you have places upon your planet which have severe drought, even as you have places upon your planet which have great floods. You have islands which are appearing in your oceans which had not been recognised before. Your scientists are seeing land masses within 10, or 15, 20 feet of the surface of your oceans which were not there previously. But because of the technology that is being used they are able to determine how far away and how deep these masses lie within the waters.

But let us alter your thinking just a little bit for a moment. Think of the effect of the alteration of the electromagnetic field. As there is an axis tilt, what effect does it have upon that which is the human species, the inhabitants of the planet? What effect does it have on the animals and on the vegetation? You who are an energy vibration which are held together, so to speak, by the magnet which is your divinity, what effect does this alteration on the electromagnetic field have upon you? Unbalance. It will accentuate the unbalance until such time as you will find it is most inconvenient and uncomfortable to be with the planet. Does that make sense? And as this is done, then there will be necessity for you to be lifted from this situation until the Earth has had an opportunity to get used to its new status, its new way, earth masses have settled and indeed receding has taken place. This is the reason for the lift off.

Now ones are saying, "When will it be, and how will it be and when will I go?" This seems to be the primary thought in most ones consciousness, is it not? "And do I get into a blue ship or a green one?" But think for a moment, you have come as volunteers, you have come as workers, does it not stand to reason in your consciousness that you will be around through the initial changes so you might assist others. And there are ones upon the planet who have volunteered to stay in physical form as the last inhabitants of the planet. So hence they will leave the planet in spirit.

Much evacuation has already begun. Think of earthquake victims, as you would call them. Think of those who have been involved in cataclysms about your planet within the past decade. These ones have had opportunity for removal, both in form and in spirit. You put great emphasis upon your physical form. I do not mean to belittle your form but it isn't of that great a significance to us, because we see your spirit and we know of your divinity. Because you do not have the recognition or understanding of experiences beyond your own physicality you are hesitant to leave that which you know and understand. And this is appreciated by us. However, if we could suggest to you that if you had chosen prior to entering your embodiment to leave your form upon the planet Earth, and to greet this experience with joy, it will be much easier for you. And if you are to come in your own form, that you know as your physical being, then that is fine also. It is not of as great a significance as you have placed upon it...

When will the axis shifts take place?

SOLTEC ...When it is time. It does not actually happen according to that which would be a date for you, but rather, it is part of a whole cycle that is going on within your dimension upon your Earth. And if you will watch of the cycle of events, how one thing follows another and follows another and follows another, then you can see how the changes come into being. That is how you can anticipate, that is how you can forecast that which you call change.

As we have spoken and it is not seen to be any different, there is a very strong possibility -- indeed, probability -- of four meteors coming to your planet by the mid point of your decade. We have the capacity to alter the course of these meteors, but we cannot do this without direct instruction from the Throne.

Is this similar to Atlantis?

SOLTEC There is a great similarity because there is a great replay in what is going on on your planet. There are many Atlanteans, if you would say, who have incarnated at this particular influx of your planet. And their point is to try to balance what they left in an unbalanced state earlier.

Is that why crystals have become popular?

SOLTEC Man has put a great deal of energy into crystals. Man has programmed crystals. Please note my careful selection of words when I say, crystalline energy is pure. However, crystals can be programmed to be used in many ways. You recognize it is the result of the use of crystals that you have the tilt on your axis that you have now.

How will the weather patterns be affected?

SOLTEC ...You are experiencing, and you have experienced great droughts in specific areas, just as other areas have experienced severe floodings, mud slides, and all of those that you would speak of. These are primarily the reaction of the geothermal blanket that is about your planet. This blanket is impacted upon by the bombardment of the rays from that which is your sun, or your source of heat. There is this constant bombardment that is going on. Part of your blanket, in your terms, has gotten holes in it. Hence, there is an intensity as this bombardment comes through, and this intensity is experienced in a reactive state, causing an increase in the melting of your polar caps which brings about a change in your weather patterns, which brings about a change in the way in which you sit upon your axis. That, coupled with the activity that is being brought about to have a stabilization as far as your ley lines are concerned, bring about a great variation in weather patterns.

We have spoken through this one and we have said, you will note that you are going into a two season period. You have winter or you have summer. You do not have those seasons that are the sliding from one to the other. For indeed, your thermal blanket is not allowing this because of the thinness and the holes that are in it.

We of the Fleet work with this to assist in the stabilization. Particularly we have ones of the Fleet that are working with the rifts in the surface of your planet that are known as your fault lines, and we are also working most intently with your ley line systems in order to assist in this stabilization process.

However, the weather patterns are influenced by that which are the thought forms, or the thought manifestations that man has put forth also. So though we may take steps, or we may assist, some patterns are set up by man himself, and it is man that has created his own droughts in some areas, and it is man that has created his own floods in some other areas.

* * * * *

Salutations Eartheons, I am Cuptan Fetogia speaking to you as a representative of the Inner Council Ring. My thoughts would be to that which are the inhabitants of the planet known as Earth.

That which is the thought form that has culminated to the point of evolution by ones of embodiment is a thought form of unbalance. We of the Council issue the mandate that the hand of Earth mans kind shall be stayed. He who would desire power over that which are his fellow man kind shall not be allowed to bring into manifestation those weapons that are of sufficient power to destroy his planet and upset the cosmic balance.

That which is the gift of the free will choice has been abused and misused, for it has not been one that has been utilized to bring the individual into a greater state of knowing. Rather, that which is the man kinds of the Emerauld has used this gift to manipulate his fellow man to gain in power over others. The intent has not been one of elevation, but has been one of control. Such use of the free will choice is merely a reflection of the slower evolvement.

These ones that seek to manipulate and control shall be stopped. Their hand shall be stayed. Man kinds shall not be allowed to destroy the planet in the galaxy of the twelfth origin. The far-reaching effects of this selfish, self-centered mode of thinking is not deemed appropriate for the cosmic evolvement. Therefore, those ones who would hold such powah (power) within their grasp shall be stayed. That which are the Intergalactic Fleets shall be given license to intercede within the ethors (ethers) of the planet and upon the face of the planet in the event that such actions of the man kinds of Earth indicate the necessity.

Any and all actions heretofore from this thought forward shall be carefully evaluated by the peers of the Cosmos. Direct intervention shall be allowed, shall be permissible, in the event that actions would endanger the balance of the planet, or the balance of the planet with its sister planets in its sun system. Those that would choose to war, those that would choose to control or dominate, shall be confined to that which is the surface activity of the planet. They shall not be allowed to endanger the total Earth populace.

The brothers of the Intergalactic Fleet may make themselves known, may intercede to terminate any such volatile and destructive actions. It shall be left to the wisdom and the knowing of the intergalactic commanders as to what steps, what actions, shall be taken to maintain a measure of balance upon the Emerauld. That which is the free will choice shall be honored by all ones as the intent of motive is a pure one. Those who would have motive less than pure shall know that they are monitored, and actions shall be taken to alter their intentions.

The Council has received the petitions of the commanders of the Intergalactic Fleet, as well as the petitions of the ones of Light upon the planet. The motive, the intent, of the thought put forth, has been carefully evaluated. It is recognized by the Council that such a step is a grave one. This step is taken with great love, concern, and purity of motive.

Therefore, we issue the mandate to ones upon the Emerauld that any action by any individual, or collection of individuals, shall have prompt intercession in the event that the motive intent is not of the highest order. Commanders of the Fleet may use their discretion as to the methods, the modes, of intervention that will bring forth the least unbalance upon the planet. The collective of Earth mans kind shall be given their opportunity to come forth along their path in that which has been determined as a reasonable manner. Those with pure motive intent shall feel no intercession, but shall become aware of those that guard their privilege of free will choice.

The Cosmos is of one of harmony. Those that would seat to unbalance this harmony shall be confined and inactivated. We hold all that is creation in its state of perfection. We hold forth the thought form that all ones will live together as brothers with no disharmony, each recognizing the gifts that are shared by his brother and the uniqueness of his own gifts. We hold the thought form that all grows into the perfection of the Source.

Is meditation the best that we can do to rid this planet of its stock pile of nuclear weapons?

HATONN Greetings, dear ones. Hatonn here. ...There are other activities in which you might engage, such as writing to your President, writing to those of your government, writing to ones of other governments. You might enter into marches or demonstrations against these nuclear warheads, these nuclear devices that are used to the detriment of mankind.

However, at this point in your cycle such outward manifestations do not bring about the desired results as quickly as those thoughts or those prayers which you project to others concerning peace and balance upon your planet. At this time these thoughts accomplish far more than those letters you would pen to your President and the leaders of your countries. For in most instances these letters do not reach the ones that need to read them, for they are carefully screened and blocked. And in some instances in the past, those that have written letters concerning disarmament, concerning the use of nuclear warheads and missiles have been harassed by their own governments.

At this point, there is much greater work for each of you to do than for you to suffer the harassment of your own government because of your interest and your desire for world peace. Projecting the thought and holding the thought accomplishes a great deal, and the thought that you project does go forth to the ones that need to receive it. This I can assure you. And we continue to receive, to feel of those thought forms that you send forth, and we add our energies with them also to assist the leaders of your government towards steps for your world peace.

Is the thinning of the ozone layers at the north and south poles a result of the atmospheric testing?

SOLTEC ...Yes and no. A lot of this thinning in the ozone layer about your planet is not only because of the nuclear testing but it is also because of the pollution about your planet -- recognizing the largest percentage of your pollution are negative thought forms. And so, you would be concerned of the smog of your various cities, you would be concerned of the emissions from your motor vehicles, etc., and there would be great emphasis on cleaning up these particular areas. You would be concerned with the pollution of the various factories, etc. But how many are working on cleaning up their thought forms? This is from a planetary view, for indeed, to remove the level of negativity that is within the thought forms would assist in the healing, shall we say, of these particular areas over your two poles.

These areas have been repaired repeatedly for many years by those of us of the Fleet. There are portions of the Fleet that are stationed in these areas and they work to weave and bring together the fragile threads of the ozone layer that are left in that area. However, they do not always, at this point in your own evolution, have what you would call 100 percent success.

There is more thinning that is anticipated over your polar areas particularly as the ecological balance is disturbed. For you recognize, with the warming that is caused by the thinning of the ozone layer there are those which are your ice caps that are melting quite rapidly. Indeed, whether you are aware or not, there are many large blocks of ice -- I believe you call them glaciers, you would call icebergs, small islands -- that are breaking loose and there is thawing that is going on beneath some of the masses. There are areas that you have considered to be land at your polar regions that you will find as this greenhouse, as this warming continues is not land but it is based on water.

Have governments been experimenting in blowing holes in the ozone so that signals could go through into the universe?

SOLTEC There is great consideration by ones of governments upon your planet to use the Cosmos, as I believe you would call it a garbage collection area. These ones are anticipating that your systems that you would call rockets and that which have propulsion that would leave your planet would be filled with debris and that which you would desire to move from your planet and released into that which you call outer space. However, we will intercede in such a situation.

The communication from your particular planet with other planetary systems does not place a hole in the ozone layer. What affects this is the thinning and the unbalance of the oxygen, carbon dioxide level upon your planet. As you remove plants, as your forests are cut down, so it is you affect the oxygen, carbon dioxide ratio on your planet. This is the great impact on the ozone layer. This is where your thinning comes about.

Your carbon dioxide level, your pollution level at this time is much greater than it was. Why? You have more animal life than you have plant life and you're very busy, you animal life, with chopping down the plant life. And so it is, you do not have that which brings about an exchange.

The explosions of your nuclear devices within the surface of your planet also affects this oxygen, carbon dioxide ratio. Those explosions which are above the surface of your planet affect the same. So it is, that delicate balance that you would call the nature's balance, that has been disturbed.

ASHTAR (adds) ...Greetings, beloved ones. Ashtar here... Your nuclear mishap (Chernobyl), your testing within your own country, and those of other countries, have a direct impact upon this (ozone) curtain -- thinning it, causing a shifting in its molecular structure, and dispersing networks of molecules that have been your protection in the past. Ones of the Fleet work most diligently and conscientiously to repair the thinning areas of your curtain, to minimize the velocity of the rays that are coming to you, so that your physical beings would be able to tolerate them.

Man on Earth was not intended to have as his source of energies, nuclear power, as he envisions it. He is destroying the atomic structure to bring forth bursts of energy, when actually he shall learn to combine energies, molecules, energy molecules, to bring him a greater energy than he knows. However, this molecular structure of which I speak is not within the realm of man in his present mode of thinking. The oil cartels, your bankers, and other industrial magnates would discourage this type of use to bring about greater energies. And indeed, there is a strong possibility that it would be perverted to selfish uses, hence this knowledge is not shared at this time.

But we say to all Earth mankind, as you lay aside your weapons, and you seek harmonious methods of dealing with you brothers upon the planet, and as you look for sound ecological means of producing energy, so shall the higher thought forms be given to you that you might learn to use the energies available to you without destroying anything upon your planet...

Mark well that which has been given to you. Look for your signs for they shall be all about you, and know that this is but a preview of that which is yet to come. How shall you handle this preview, man of Earth? The choice is yours. Should you choose the path of Light, we stand ever ready to assist you, to guide your steps and to come to your assistance. We stand as your brothers of the stars to walk with you into your next phase of development, into that which you speak of as the New Day.

To all Light workers may I send forth the thought form of our love and our joy as we work with you. You have selected a task that is great in comparison to that which we do. We salute you in your endeavors, and we join with you in expressing our love and our adoration for the Radiant One.

Do the nuclear blasts set off by such ones as the U.S., Russia and France affect the tectonic plates so that earthquakes then occur?

SOLTEC ...Indeed, there is a relationship, my brother. There is a great relationship. For if you would think of it, you have plates that cover the outer surface of your planet and these plates ordinarily would ride side by side and there would be a small measure in which one might overlap a little. And then again, it might be that they would come apart some for this is a breathing process, so to speak.

When you let off that which you would call your nuclear explosions, you are disrupting an atomic pattern -- for you would not desire to do this as a coming together but rather as a splitting. So it is not a harmonious blast to start with -- it is brought about from disruption or unbalance. It would go into the planet and because all atoms are interrelated, that unbalance that is within your blast is experienced by the atomic structure of your planet because there is a consciousness that goes from one atom to the other atom to the other atom of all creation, and it is particularly accelerated when you would get into specific of your -- I believe you would call them your chemicals or that which is the makeup. So, the atomic structure of your planet is immediately affected because it receives that which is not of balance. You add to that the impact of the explosion which accentuates and accelerates this unbalance...

In the places that you have mentioned -- that which is your own United States, in your own continent, that which is known to you as the Russian country and that which is known to you as the French country -- these are released on areas that have fault lines themselves. And so, it immediately causes -- when there is an explosion here -- it immediately causes this plate over here to go up on this one or down on it creating an acceleration in pressure. This, in turn, brings about that which you would call a quaking because it is that the plates are trying to get into some sort of a balance because the atomic structure of each plate is out of balance.

You are not aware of the number of quakings that go on about your planet, for indeed, there are several each of your 24 hour periods and you do not hear of these. For they would seem minor to your scientists and yet in some instances upon your planet, these quakings are your plates coming into a balance together.

That which is known as your San Francisco quake was brought about because there was an override of one plate over another and this was called a fault line. The idea, shall we say, would be that this plate would shift this way. Then you would have a balance between the two plates. However, because of the nuclear explosions you went this way (opposite direction) which caused increased pressure on the other side of this plate. This plate was caused from sitting this way. When the move came about it caused this side of this plate to tip downward. Hence, it went under this plate which I believe you would call your New Madrid fault line. And as it went under, this one rode on the top and so it is, this side of the plate then has impact. And so it is, we would go around your world.

Does this splitting of the atom affect the length of the cycle we are in?

MONKA You of Earth are involved in several cycles. A cycle here might be defined as a chain of events, as a chain of circumstances where one step follows the next to achieve the next. If the choice is to try to skip part of the steps then the time in earthly terms is shortened. I shall use here briefly an example.

Your scientists on Earth have developed the ability to split the atom. They have not been content with those atomic structures that are not living structures. But they have turned to your living elements, consequently, your hydrogen bomb. The living elements are elements that are felt, that are utilized throughout the universe. Thus, there is a chain or a molecular reaction continually between and among all molecules, all atoms involving hydrogen. When this atom is split and there is an explosion upon your earth involving the hydrogen atom, this is felt throughout the universe. There is a decided unbalance. There is a decided reverberation that is felt throughout the universe. Indeed, in such an instance it is as if the universe contracts and shudders in the horror of the activity. This shortens the cycle, for it burns up and destroys that which is living and is not to be touched.

It was mentioned earlier about sending "debris" into outer space. Was this referring in some part to the disposal of nuclear waste?

HATONN As Earth and Earth man continues on his present course he shall not be in a position that he will be using nuclear energy in vast quantities. For though Earth man has this ability he has chosen in his activity with the atoms and with the elements to use these in a destructive manner rather than constructive one. He has chosen to manufacture weapons and warheads. As you of Earth would split the atom, as your phrase is used, you release an energy into the ethers, into the Universe that is unbalanced and unresolved because you have violated that element. As you do this the ethers about Earth are caused to bubble, to boil. There is a seething that is about Earth as a result of this. We, of the Fleet, have worked most diligently to see that this is encapsulated around your planet. There has been, and here I hesitate that I might use a word that is familiar to you ones of Earth -- I would choose the word veil -- a walled veil or a veiled wall has been placed around the energies to contain them within the ethers of the Earth that they not go forth into the rest of the Universe, that they might cause unbalance there. This we cannot allow. For balance and harmony shall be maintained throughout the Universe, irrespective of the scientists upon Earth.

They have no place to bury this waste. This is what concerns me.

HATONN And they shan't. No, they shall find no way to dispose of this within the Earth, for this material cannot be disposed of within the Earth, in your earthly words, "safely and securely." For these energies cannot be neutralized, cannot be stopped because that action which has initiated your nuclear energy has violated the elements, the atomic structure of the elements that are involved. And this violation shall be contained within the ethers of Earth that it cannot go forth to the rest of the Universe.

No, your ones have not found a way to dispose of these wastes, and in the days to come they shall not, for they have stepped over, they have trespassed a Law which they had no right to trespass. And so they are reaping the consequences. You, Earth man are reaping the consequences of their actions.

It was mentioned earlier about the nuclear accident at Chernobyl. There was a cloud of radioactive material formed. What about this cloud?

MONKA ...There are many ones upon your planet that have a great concern regarding the cloud coverage that holds the radioactive components. Be aware that regardless of where the cloud goes, or of where the rainfall is, or how the nuclear components return to Earth, they will be felt throughout the planet. For there has been an elemental, as well as an ecological imbalance. Those individuals, those hu-mans, that have been in close proximity to the area, will display the symptoms of this closeness in the not too distant day. There are ones upon your planet now that are rejoicing at the minimum of casualties, and the non-serious manifestations for hu-man-kind. Their rejoicing shall be quite sobered in not too many days.

Just as ones have felt of this incident according to their proximity, there are ones throughout the Cosmos that are feeling of the unbalance, that are feeling of this nuclear reaction. Ships, our ships have been called forth in concentration to help to stabilize, and to minimize the involvement of the cloud activities. Indeed the cloud has been, as you would say, "seeded" that it might return its radioactive material to Earth in areas that are not as heavily populated. We have done this in an attempt to assist you of Earth.

There have been ones upon your planet that have indeed seemed quite unconcerned of the whole affair, for it has not been in their own front yard. As you are aware this brings forth a great heaviness for us at one's lack of concern for his fellow man. Man of Earth must recognize that he is not an isolated being on Earth, but his well being is dependent upon the actions, the thoughts, the deeds of all others. And just as he is dependent upon them, so do his actions, his deeds, his thoughts have impact upon all ones on planet Earth.

If I could leave one thought with you, this is the thought, this is the seed that I would plant within your consciousness -- that you have impact on all of Earth, just as all ones of Earth have impact upon you.

I shall not delve into numbers or degree of evolvement in this nuclear incident for as you have been told before those that are involved have volunteered to be there. As these situations become more evident on your planet may I suggest to you that as you become aware of them, that you bless these that have come to share in an attempt to assist all of mankind. Bless these ones, these volunteers for that which they have come to do.

KEILTA Greetings in the Light of the Radiant One. ...We shall be coming in closer to your Earth's surface than we have heretofore in an attempt to assist in the neutralization of the nuclear fallout that is about your planet. We are aware that you are concerned of the irradiation fallout from the nuclear plant of Chernobyl. This is primarily because of your knowledge of this plant. There is even greater danger to all ones upon your planet because of the underground testing of your nuclear devices that many of the countries, including your own are currently involved in.

Each of your countries is aware of the activity of the other and uses this as a justification to continue their own ignition of varying devices. Just as this releases radioactivity in your air and your ethers it also releases the same within your earth surface, causing damage to the Earth, to the ground that you walk on, as well as to the waters, with not to mention the great impact it has upon your weather patterns.

Quietly and without your awareness the governments of your planet have released much radioactive material into your ethers. This is part of our mission as we come in close, is to assist in the neutralization of some of these energies. We also are endeavoring to make our presence known in an invitation to ones of governments to acknowledge our presence and invite us to be involved with them in the governmental process upon your planet.

Can you give us an overview of some of the things you are doing to help stabilize Mother Earth?

SARNA ...Let us speak first of the maintenance program that is in operation about your planet. We have squadrons of ships that have the responsibility of working within the grid systems and the electromagnetic fields of the planet to hold the Earth in its present orbital pattern. They work with all of the major fault lines about the face of the Earth Mother. Never, I repeat, never are you left unattended.

The ability of the Earth Mother to hold any major stabilization on her own at this time is quite unlikely. She is too weak within her own electromagnetic conjunction and has released sufficiently that she no longer desires to remain in this pattern.

No we are not trespassing a universal law because we are doing this to allow her to release of this vibrational frequency as well as prepare for the new one. She has been weakened by all the release of the Earth man as he has raped and pillaged of her and dumped his excesses physically and in thought form upon her. She is weak. We work to help give her strength to maintain a short period longer. This period is to allow mankind upon her surface to grow to his own graduation.

The major San Andreas fault did not involve itself in the recent earthquake on your coastal line (San Francisco, Oct.17, 1989). It was a line that was used to release some of the pressure much as a tributary takes the overflow of the waters of the large river. But see how this one that is a tributary can cause such a change in the surface of the land. See of the change and the evident paralyzation that has been caused as man must search for new routes and new locations. The shifting of the plates and the manner of the shifting is most significant. Be aware of this.

The tributary has taken a portion of the impact, but the greater impact is still there. This release was a demonstration to man, an effort to alleviate the pressure with a minimal of damages upon the surface. It was the first blast upon the trumpet that sounds the alarm.

I am speaking of the earthquake that is so close to you within the U.S. of A. But have any of you directed your attention to the quaking in other parts of your planet? Are you aware of the great release from physical for many ones? Are you aware of the change in the geophysical structures in those areas? Have you even suspected that this earth rumblings have been used as an opportunity for bringing ones up and for putting ones of the Fleet down? Indeed, even in the quake along your western coast, both of these activities were accomplished. We have taken on the form of man to assist man. We have entered into the form of man to assist him

47

during this upcoming period. Know, during each acknowledged disaster, ones are released from their bondage and
ones of us come in to shore up the quaking Light working
force. We come to work beside you to bring about the
planetary changes necessary for the New Day.

Would you comment on what we are doing to Earth's environment?

SARNA ...I would like to take a moment, with your permission, that we would explore this, for this is an issue which
affects each one of you who are on the planet.

Those ones who are called your scientists are not
being recognized. Their voice is not being heard when they
speak of some of the problems: As far as your ozone layers;
as far as the difficulties with the air which you breathe. As
you become more and more aware you will note there is a
chain or a link with all of Creation upon your planet. And you
deplete one portion of it, or you get it to such a state that it
can no longer function in its capacity, and it has impact on the
rest of the chain.

There is one word which covers the consciousness of
the collective on planet Earth; and for that collective it is
called "power" and "greed." They would look at, for example,
your forest, and they would not see of its beauty; they would
not see of its allowment of life; they would not see how these
trees impact upon each individual upon the planet. But
rather, they see the signs of monies. This is a serious
problem. You have your pollution of your cities by your conveyances which put forth great unbalanced belches of
smoke. And as we observe patterns about your planet we
see pockets of great density. We see pockets which at one
time had been quite clear which are coming in and becoming
quite hazy. And ones within these pockets of places would
say, "We have done no thing to cause this haziness to appear." But "we" is the collective consciousness called Earth

mankind, and that "we" has done things. And this is coming off.

You have had that, and you are having that which are the release of some of your nuclear places which are releasing energies which are caught on your winds, which are being deposited in areas on opposite sides of the planet. These things you know; you are aware of. But I ask you, are you as individuals trying to help? These unbalances can be a reason that there can be a great mutation in that which is called the form of Earth mankind. As your level of noxious gases increases you will find you will have to go underground into that which is an artificial environment, for survival. It is happening most quickly.

Similar things have happened on your planet before. And please note, I underscore similar, for they are not exact. You have not been this foolish before on this planet. But there has been an unbalance; there have been clouds which have covered the planet, which has caused a mutation in the beings.

Let each voice be heard on behalf of your planet, in that which is the yard, your garden. Do this in a loving way, that it is a haven for balance. Look seriously at that which would be the sorting of your goods and their disposal. It has come to the place it is not longer the sole responsibility of your cartels, but it rests with each one of you. And you as individuals have impact on the cartels and what they would do.

If you are living in an apartment for instance, how can you repay or give to Mother Earth that which you have taken?

SARNA ...May I say, my sister that this is a very apt question. For there are many ones that shall read of our words and these are ones that you would call apartment dwellers. To be able to share with Mother Earth does not require a great field or a great space. Rather it is an acknowledgment

49

of that which she shares with you and that which she gives to you. As you would gaze from you window, or you would step from your door, you would look about and you would know that which you see is Mother Earth. Yes, in some instances her surface has been covered by roads. There have been buildings that have been placed upon her surface. But there are also areas that have green grasses and small flowers and beautiful trees that peek through these areas. These are your examples of the fields that are just beyond your reach.

Your greatest communion with Mother Earth is to love her, and to let her know that you love her; and that you feel with her; and that you are grateful to her for all that she gives to you. You do not have to have great fields that you would adore or that you would romp through. You do not have to have great patches of soil. But rather as you would see the beauty of Mother Earth wherever this beauty might lie that you would acknowledge this consciously and thank her for sharing and allowing you the opportunity to be.

What can we do regarding the acid rain?

SARNA ...There are many sadnesses that have come upon your planet as man has attempted to use his technology.

You have been told on numerous occasions to hold your planet in love, to see it in the golden bubble of love in its highest perfection. This is something that each of you can do each hour of your day. This thought that is projected by you, individually and collectively, literally dispels clouds of negativity or of harm, of harmful substance that would come to you. The projected thought is a very powerful tool that you have not fully implemented.

In addition to holding this thought, individually and collectively, work with ones of your governments, of your departments -- and here I scan for the proper term,-- but work with others, individually and collectively, to remove the negativity that is about your planet.

As the ethers are being or have been cleared about your planet, there has been a fallout to the planet of the negative thought forms from the other dimensions. These are manifesting in various ways that are observable by you at this time. You will note of new terms, new conditions that are coming into your awareness. These are thought forms that are manifesting for you, within your dimension. Work with others to minimize, or to eliminate these with specific emphasis on the process that has initiated the condition. But above all, may I ask of each of you, may I strongly urge you and all ones upon the planet to hold your beloved planet in Light and love, for this can do great miracles.

In the construction business when the trees are torn down or moved, does this bring about negativity for Mother Earth?

MONKA ...Certainly that which you do does not assist Mother Earth at this time.

Do you recognize that as your trees and your forests are diminished that so it is that your oxygen supply is affected. Many of you have forgotten that it is through your plants that you have a continuous and a fresh supply of oxygen. There has been current businesses upon your planet that have chosen to go in and destroy the great rain forests upon your planet. This reduces your amount of oxygen by one third. May I suggest to all ones that have the place and to those of you that would have the desire, to plant trees for these beautiful creatures assist in the transmutation of negative energy upon your planet, for they take in the vibrations that are heavier, that are more dense, and they transmute these into ones that are of a finer attunement. In addition, on your physical plane they also assist in bringing about the balance and the needed oxygen for your planet.

Mother Earth's face has been changed many times by Earth man for Earth man feels a great need to alter that which you would consider the natural landscape because of buildings, because of roads. In the New Day, which is fast approaching for you, there shall not be need for roads for you shall travel in a different manner. Your buildings shall be built on location that harmonize with your natural environment rather than alter it.

At this point within the cycle, to return to your question, you do not increase the negativity, for Mother Earth no longer assumes this. But as you go about your daily toil, recognize that you are altering Mother Earth's face. Bless her and ask her permission that you might do this that she is given consideration. As you freely do this so shall she offer up her blessings to you, and so shall you feel the warmness within your heart as you know you have included her in that which is going on.

Can you tell us about time capsules that were buried during the Lemurian and Atlantean times, and how soon we will become aware of their contents?

SARNA There is knowledge within these which will assist Earth mankind in an accelerated growth and awareness. ("So that should be soon?") What is "soon?" It will not be before Earth mankind is ready for the trust. When this happens, it will come as a great surprise, for indeed, the time capsules, if you would use this term, which have placed within them specific teachings of ancient and cosmic origin are not capsules at all. They are crystalline scrolls or chips, if you would call this, that have been carefully stored, placed in safe places in various places about your planet.

In order to assure Earth mankind does not have the opportunity to enter into his present pattern or a repetition of his present pattern, all of the pieces must come together in order to have the understanding. For each is incomplete within itself. Do you understand?

More or less. I am wondering if this was buried during Lemuria or Atlantis times, then you are saying that now these same things will not happen to the Earth at the present time, yet we have been told that the Earth is going to go through cleansing. Isn't that the same idea as what happened to Atlantis and Lemuria?

SARNA If you would look at it solely from the cleansing, you would say yes, that a cleansing has gone forth previously. But recognize the result of the cleansing and the level, if you would desire to use that word, of entity who will be the inhabitant of the Earth, and the cleansing as you would say, or the disruption, or alteration, perhaps would be a more accurate term, of the geophysical face of the Earth Mother will enable some of these time capsules, as you would call them, to come to the awareness of man. Otherwise, it would not be possible.

That which would come to the awareness of man prior to the Earth changes, is but the appetizer for the banquet. For there are those who come close to understanding some specific knowledge that is still contained within some of the pyramids that are upon your planet. However, that is but the appetizer.

Recognize also your pyramids... upon your plane now are not that which you see upon the surface. There is a pyramid that is below that which has the same form, the same shape -- ("In the physical?") -- in the physical. ("Do they know this?") It is suspected, but it has not been documented on your plane.

And what is this when you would see it? Have you not been given the diamond as a symbol of the New Age? But as you would look at half of it, that is incomplete, you only have half the picture, do you not? As above, so below. But man has seen only that which is above the surface. And he has also removed this part (capstone) for he has removed that so he truly has an incomplete... But recognize the capstone which is made out of a material which has copper, gold, and a substance beyond your dimension, is a receiver to allow energies to come in. And as that happens, so it is the intensity is magnified within the widest part of your diamond, and its focus is down in this which also could be called a capstone (at the bottom of the "diamond"). It is called the base stone, which again sends it forth and out. And each side of your pyramid then receives and is as a screen, if you would say, that would send out the energy. ("Much like an antenna.") Yes. This could be as your dish, it broadcasts it out...

As you recognize this, the energies come to you in a pulsing manner. The energies do not "rain" upon you, but it is a universal pulse that would come. And so you would have a pulse that would come, and that pulse then would come here, and it then would go out. Now this portion of your pyramids are lined.

Externally they are made of the stone even as the top portion is, but there is a lining in them that is as a conductor. In order for man not to blow it, there was set forth first that which is a material which would be similar to your lead, similar to but not exactly as, that was placed at this line... It is beneath the Earth's surface. Then from there you have Earth and then you have that which is the floor of the pyramid, or which is acknowledged.

Now recognize this is several feet deep, so you have that which you would say chambers which are being opened up, or discovered, and you have yet to reach this level because man is not ready for that. Man is not ready for that.

Where are the capstones that are missing from the pyramids?

SARNA There was this structure that originally was in your temple, the early temples of Lemuria and Atlantis, because it was felt the intensification. And the exalted ones would have chambers in the top in which they would have a closer, more intense communion. The capstone was never anchored. It merely was there as a receiver and it was in place that it might vibrate according to the energy in-flow. Also, it was sufficient space, shall we say, that ones could enter from other dimensions, for your capstone area could be as large as your room you are in now. And ones felt at the time one of your civilizations was going through its difficulty or its growing pains, they felt that in order to receive they must have this unique combination of elements and so ones felt they could steal the capstones and they could have them for themselves alone -- again, isolation -- again, having a "one-ups-manship" on the brothers that inhabit the planet with you.

And so it was ones attempted to remove these, to take them and to hide them. In your terms this was a "no no" so they merely were dissolved, disintegrated, whatever term you would use. And the etheric remains there now, the etheric capstone, if you will, is still there. This is why the pyramids have stayed intact, is because of the etheric capstone that is on them. The original receivers will precipitate from the etheric ones when this can be done in such a manner that it will not bring unbalance to the consciousness of Earth mankind. But first Earth mankind will need to get used to the idea that we are around and we can bring things into manifestation, into being within your dimension, and we can replace or regenerate those which have been removed.

Selfishness has played much of a lead role on your planet, the selfishness and self-centeredness within the individual. Those who were the kings, the regents who were buried within these structures were desired to be there for they felt this was the quickest way for ascension because of the energy that is contained within.

There is great emphasis placed upon the pyramids in the country that is known to you as Egypt, but recognize you have great pyramids within that which is South America and that which is your Central America. And there are magnificent ones beneath the surface of your waters...

If you will look, one day you will see there is a belt about that which is your equator now, and that which would go from your North Pole to your South Pole -- so you have a band this way (horizontally) and you have a band this way (vertically). And within those areas -- and I will not give you within six miles or five miles one way or the other -- but there is a pattern of energy pyramids that assist in the stabilization of your planet.

Is that where some of the time capsules are?

SARNA These do not have that which you would call time capsules within them...

Most of the time capsules, that which you speak, would be considered in earthen vaults, not specifically within the pyramid areas. But within these structures (pyramids) you will note there is writing that is not truly understood by man upon your planet. He thinks he understands and he thinks he knows the language, however, it is not a language with which he is familiar. It tells him how to get here (the bottom half of the pyramid which is below the surface). Within this portion there are teachings, if you will, on the walls within vault like structures which have preserved them, which will unlock specific secrets -- and that is such a delicious word for you -- certain not understood portions of your own evolvement and connection cosmically. Also, within some there are those which will have various lessons for you in, shall we say, the manufacture of specific metals or the components of specific metals that are adaptable and pliable for cosmic travel. There are those which are knowledge that you might keep your form young and beautiful. There is knowledge of a, shall we say, eternal beauty. There is knowledge of eternal strength. All of this information that would be considered dimensionally expanding is available within the vaults and within the teachings of the pyramids...

We understand the civilizations of Lemuria and Atlantis had reached a higher development than now, and yet supposedly the energies are higher now than they were then?

JOKHYM In the Radiance of the Source, I greet you. ...The spirituality upon your planet at the time of these eras that you speak was not the same. For man, and here I use this term as Earth man, had not evolved to the same state as you are in your evolutionary process now. Man had, because of his association with brothers of different stars and galaxies, attained a high degree of scientific knowledge. However, his spirituality was limited. Indeed, there was a small number of ones within Lemuria and Atlantis, as you would choose to call these, that were very spiritually evolved. However, the knowledge that they had, that they had received, the teachings they had received were guarded well as mysteries and not shared with the masses. The priests and priestesses were looked upon as ones with great powers because they did know the secrets that were brought from the other stars and the other galaxies, the other dimensions. Scientific endeavor at that time was different than your scientific endeavor now. For there was a great utilization of ley lines. There was a greater utilization of crystalline energy. Ones could transmit thought more easily than is done in your period. However, man, Earth man in toto had not evolved to the same degree that you on your planet at this time have reached.

Ones that inhabit a planet must go through an evolutionary process. You are reaching a heightened, or height, top height for your dimension, as you would prepare to move into the next one. At the time of Lemuria, at the time of Atlantis you were not at the height of your dimensional parameters. For you had not evolved sufficiently to reach that state. You have grown in your scientific knowledge. Great secrets, if you would choose to use that word, have been shared with man on Planet Earth to allow him to evolve, to assist him in his evolvement. Unfortunately man has used some of this knowledge in ways that would wage war and would suppress others.

So to reply to your question, you have reached a higher level of evolution than you experienced in those eras. Each time, if you would choose to use this word, that there is another rotation, another evolution for your planet it is at a higher level of consciousness and awareness than the one that was experienced previously.

Concerning the possible openings in the pyramids of Giza, is this a part of information that will come forth to help the energies to raise on Earth now?

SARNA ...There is nothing, there is no thing that is going on upon your planet at this time that is by accident. For there is a fine tuning process that is being experienced that will help to bring an enlightenment to Earth man kind. The concern that is being expressed is that specific ones are taking one small piece of information and they are drawing this as the sole conclusion, to the exclusion of the other pieces that would assist them.

May I take this opportunity to suggest to all ones to be open, to allow thoughts to flow through you that you would grow in a greater understanding.

This which is known as your pyramid is but one of many which are at specific points about your planet that are used as balancing devices in connection with the energies that are put forth from specific ships to assist in Earth's balance upon her axis. Within each one of these pyramids is a specific portion of information, is a specific locked teaching. It is not until each of the pyramids is recognized, and there are seven of them upon your planet, that the whole key will be known. For it is as this one's mysteries are unlocked, so it is that guidance can be received that will guide ones to other pyramids that are not known to you on your Earth's surface at this time.

I would add a thought here. Of a long distant day ago, your Earth sat straight upon its axis. But indeed, as that which is known to you as negativity crept in, there has been an unbalance, an unbalance to the point you could have toppled. And alas, this would have had a total cosmic effect that was quite undesirable. And so it is that the ships of the Ashtar Command have come forth. And there are ones that have formed, as you would say, a magnetic belt about your planet. And they are linked individually and collectively with specific pyramids upon your planet. And as the energies are emitted, and they are pulsed back, so it is that we assist you in maintaining a relative state of stability.

Where does the Bermuda Triangle fit into the picture?

HATONN This particular place on your globe is the seat of a large pyramid which houses a large crystal that is influenced by, as well as influencing, our beams from our ships, your moon and the energies that come forth at various times of your history. This is a portion of your continent that is known to you as Atlantis.

In future days this area shall rise up from its salty wet sleep to be part of the virgin new soil that will hold your seeds and sprout your vegetation. This pyramid will come forth and shine in its magnificence and beauty. You ones of the new age, the new day, will see of this and you will learn how to use the energy of this crystal within this pyramid, as well as others, to navigate your globe as well as visit other parts of your universe...

Are some of the standing stone sites, such as Stonehenge, located at node points on ley lines to act similar to the system described for preventing or minimizing the vibrations that are currently underway in and about the planet?

SARNA ...Indeed these points are connecting points which when fully operational can set up an attunement which goes about your planet. Do you know when you would strike a tuning fork and it can be used to strike another and another and another, so it is when these points -- including some of the pyramidal structures that are currently below the waters and some of the other structures that are below the waters and have not been acknowledged; those even above the waters which have not been acknowledged -- it would be when they are in fully operational condition that you would touch these and it would be as if you are setting up a tuning upon about your planet...

Could you explain more about the grid system, the ley lines that go around this planet and in the planet please?

SOLTEC ...If you would, visualize for a moment your planet from where we see it. See it as vibrating, moving lines of energy that are all interconnected. You think of your grid pattern as that which is one dimension, but recognize your grids, your ley lines go across, and they go up and down, and they go at angles. And it is that these are patterns, or pathways for energy flow.

There are those lines, if you would use this term, that have been inactive, shall we say. And there are ones that are sent in various places perhaps to activate these, for they would allow a specific energy to be infused into an area through them to awaken a particular energy or ley line. These lines carry energy vibrations.

Recognize that when you would come to a space in which you have lines that are running on one plane, and then there would be that which would be perpendicular to it, there is that which is created as an etheric window. And it is through these etheric windows that ships go in and out from one dimension to another. So hence, there are many windows. Now recognize also that these windows not only have to do with the face of your planet, but they are within your planetary's, beneath its surface. And so, I see not that which is a ball, as you would say, or an egg that is sitting within the Cosmos, but I see a series of energy lines that are interconnected in a specific pattern and vibration that may be translated as that which is your planet.

I also see these lines going out from your planet, bringing about an inter-planetary connection, both within your sun system, your galaxy, and on to other galaxies. For see this grid system not only with your planet, but see as it grows and it expands and it reaches out, that there are pathways through which the energy may flow in a specific pattern that will bring about a specific vibration, a specific density. Hence, you have what you would call your planet Earth...

If one has a piece of property with two ley lines on it, would it be beneficial to put a medicine wheel or a pyramid between these to enhance their energy pattern?

BEATRIX Greetings beloveds... It is with joy that I again return. In reply to your question my brother, I would suggest to you a medicine wheel. For these ley lines of which you speak have to do with an ancient heritage pattern that must be manifested in this particular area upon this property. There are ones that will be attracted to this area after the balancing has taken place -- the balancing which will be created by the wheel. And they shall be afforded the opportunity to share a deep teaching that will be a portion of that which another has already been given. This is my reason for the suggestion of the wheel instead of the pyramid.

Recognize upon your planet, as you have ley lines that they play a specific role. Specific currents flow with and through the ley lines to create a pattern that encapsulates your planet. Indeed, it creates a specific energy field about your planet. Those that were known to you as the original race of your country knew well of the ley lines and what was used or practiced in specific areas. This information has been buried. In some instances it is as if it were forgotten though it has not been forgotten, it has merely been put way aside. Just by the mere fact that this thought, this question, has come to your consciousness is an indication that there is now a need for this portion of information to be brought into focus and given or shared with one that has another portion.

There is much that must be done yet upon your planet to assist in bringing about the utilization of all the forces that are available to you. Ones have volunteered from within the Cosmos to be energy carriers about your planet. These ones are laying specific grid patterns that connect specific ley lines and energy flows which shall be utilized upon your planet in the future for healing, for crop production, for travel, for levitation, and for manifestation...

I would like to know more about and the purposes of the energy vortexes, particularly those located in the Southwest?

HATONN ...May I begin my reply with a qualification. There are energy vortexes all around your planet. It is at this time, because of the history, the knowledge, the attunement of that which is known as your American Indian, and too, because this is an area of your country that is relatively unsettled in comparison with other portions of your country, that these particular vortexes have come into much more awareness at this time.

As you would gaze at the grid lines about your planet you would be aware that there are specific energy patterns that flow about your planet. Some of these are well known to you. Others are yet to come into your conscious awareness. These ones that you speak of are a result of what is beneath the surface of your planet in that particular area. If you would draw a line about your globe, you would find there would be a great similarity in the latitude of these vortexes and the energy patterns of the structures that are known as your pyramids. Indeed, beneath the earth's surface in this area there are still crystals within pyramids that are active in establishing, in maintaining an energy flow about your planet.

These were brought into manifestation during the Atlantean period. These were used as methods of travel about your planet, as well as bringing into a concentrated flow sufficient energies that would allow ones of that period to be able to project a vehicle from your planet out into that which you know as the Cosmos.

This energy vortex, these energy vortexes are still in combination with energy beam patterns with other planets within your galaxy. It is part of a universal energy grid pattern. Just as the energies there are in relation to the energies of the pyramid, in that which is known as Egypt, so it is that you also have pyramidal structures in the country that is known as Mexico that is in a close approximation to this area that is known as the energy vortexes...

In the coming earth changes are their certain areas that might be safer than others? For example, what about the state of Ohio?

SARNA ...How safe do you want to be? There shall be changes about your planet, and it shall be in varying ways throughout the planet. There are those of you that have experienced earthquakes that have not experienced them in hundreds of years in specific areas upon your planet. Recognize that these changes shall not all come at one fell swoop through the planet, but they shall start out in a gradual manner. Here again, it shall be according to Earth man's reaction, Earth man's desire, Earth man's way, Earth man's whatever term you would use, as to the severity of these changes.

If Earth man should choose -- and this is a very unlikely situation, and I would say this because I know of the

Light that is on planet Earth -- but if Earth man would choose to say, "Forget it. I shall be totally involved on the material plane. I shall desire no spiritual evolvement. There is no such thing as any of this. I will only believe that which is of my senses and that which is here before me." -- if all of Earth man were to make such a comment, then Atlantis and Lemuria could both abruptly appear upon your planet. Indeed, the whole topography could be greatly altered in a matter of that which you would call less than one year. However, this is not the case with Earth man because there are Lighted ones upon the planet. And the Light is there. And it is there in areas that you are not aware of.

As we would gaze upon the planet, the Light centers -- and that's what each of you are, are Light centers -- are scattered about the Emerauld as diamonds. For you are about the planet. And there are ones that have taken on embodiment in that which you would call adult form without going through the birthing process or that which you know as childhood, in order to be assistors in maintaining the Light within the planet.

You would ask of your state. There shall be modifications. There shall be changes within your state, but these shall not be the same as those that will be felt in other states. However, because of the manner of lifestyle that you within your country have developed, you are very dependent on one another. And so that which would effect one portion of your country shall be greatly felt in all other portions of the country. So from that perspective, you will feel the changes acutely. However, regardless of how acute you feel the changes, you may find that the actual change within your specific location may not be as great as it is in other areas. But you will feel them nonetheless, because you are interconnected.

And what about the state of California?

SOLTEC ...Even as I would speak with you this hour, there

64

is council going on within the chambers that is closely monitoring the activities of Mother Earth, the planet in toto. We have evacuated ones from Inner Earth as a protective measure for the upcoming changes that shall be about the face of your planet. However, at this hour, I cannot give you a specific date, a specific time. But what I can give you is an increased awareness that you might tune to yourselves to what you feel, to what you are experiencing, that you might watch what is going on about you.

Do you watch the small ones that are known as your squirrels? Have they begun to store foods? And what of your birds? Are your migratory patterns shorter than they were? What of your trees, your foliage? Is it changing earlier, is it changing later? And what of the quaking and the trembling that you experience beneath your feet. Watch of these.

Currently, within that area that you would call your state of California, Lighted ones have come, and these are ones that would carry a great Light with them. And their purpose is to quietly administer to Earth, and assist in the balancing of the plates beneath the surface, that you would have an increased period for ones to come into their awareness and to come into a state of balance. No, I am sorry, I cannot give you date or time, for I can merely give you specifics as far as the steps of cycles in that which we anticipate...

Those of you that would have a desire to put up your stored foods, to do so now. For it is anticipated at this particular council, that great, specific geophysical, as well as Earth man changes, are coming much more quickly than had been anticipated.

There are some of you that are aware there was a prediction that there was to be a great and a mighty earthquake on the seventeenth day of your month of August (1987). And indeed, much of that which is known as California would now be beneath the surface of the waters of your

Pacific Ocean. This did not come about because the sequence that was given was accurate, however, the specific date was an inaccurate one because dates cannot be given. We can merely give you that which is the cycle of events.

Watch. Be aware that the cosmic clock has been speeded up fifteen years of your time. I have given you a key. I trust you have accepted the key...

And the area known as the Grand Canyon?

SARNA ...I would take this opportunity to speak of the location and the importance of this location, of this "natural wonder" of your planet. As you know this area is put aside that man cannot alter its face or content. Do you recognize the reason for this? This area is the coming together and the over slide area of several plates of the face of your planet. Do you realize that the impact in this area is felt in countries on the opposite side of your planet? There is an interplay of all the plates and the fault lines of your country.

Ones go to this place of earthly beauty and feel the beauty of the place. They do not dump their unwanted energies there as in your place of abode (Sedona), but rather they marvel at the earth and its beauty. Man has not been allowed to desecrate this place. It has been maintained by him for all to enjoy and experience. There are several major reasons for this. The first is there are vast deposits of minerals and their wealth beneath the surface of this place. Man is not to exploit these riches for they are to be available for another time, one of sharing and of beauty. The second reason is the importance of the location in relation to the major plates of your planet's surface.

Even as ones have put their concentration upon the San Francisco quake and the well known San Andreas fault line, have you given thought to the fault line that is known to you as the New Madrid? It too is in a most precarious state. It is in far greater position to come into physical view or have a major quake than the one of your western coast...

Please note, as you shift your attention and your thoughts to one specific place upon your planet you cause increase shifting in the hold upon the axis. Man of Earth has not yet learned the power of his thoughts. A stable thought pattern can and does do much to assist Earth at this critical time. All men of Earth have been given warning of the upcoming changes. All ones are aware of the changing times. See that which is going on about you, but maintain a stable position within your own force field...

Even as your media puts great emphasis upon specifics that happen on your planet, know as each one of you watches, reads or listens to the report that a great shifting of energies are experienced on your planet. When you can learn to listen, hear or read with no emotional output but rather a balanced thought then you are for a great good for yourselves and the planet.

But to return to your place of the Canyon. As plates come together and have the opportunity to slide and overlap according to the planetary needs, so it is that this area plays a far greater role than its merely scenic beauty...

Will catastrophic events, like the earthquake in San Francisco in 1989, be affecting us here in Montreal, Canada?

SOLTEC ...That which you ask is already happening. For there is a constant tremor level along the western shore of your continent. You will find also there is an increase in the number of tremors which are being experienced on the other coastline as well. But I would suggest to you to be concerned not of the tremors, but of the water level. Perhaps this would need a more closer monitoring than it has received heretofore...

Please comment on England and the geophysical changes that are due to happen?

SOLTEC ...What of these ones which you call the Isles? What level of consciousness do they represent? What is their connection as far as the total evolvement of Earth mankind upon your plane? Are these ones part of an outcropping of Atlantis? Is this a mountain area in which ones escaped, shall we say, when there were geophysical changes at that point? And have these ones come to balance or to save, to preserve? Are they custodians of a certain part that will be introduced? Or is it that they have been ones who have balanced out their own patterns and they are yet to experience a newness because they are balanced? These are questions which you would consider as you would think of geophysical and weather pattern changes within specific areas...

Recognize there are geophysical changes which are going on, which will be going on. Even now, you have islands which are appearing in oceans which are being recorded by your scientists as there are Earth shifts and there are shifts in the plates along the face of the Earth...

How will the three axis shifts and other geophysical changes affect Australia?

SOLTEC ...And what is meant by the shift of the axis? It is going to get a little warmer (in Australia), I would say. Recognize your planet sits at an angle. And as you have the changes, you have a shifting... So the Equator, or that which you will call your equatorial belt, will move; it will change according to where the center is of your planet.

As we observe it at this time, the electromagnetic North Pole and that which is considered by you as the North Pole are going to come more into a balance. And then again, you shall have an unbalance from it.

But, in relationship to that which is your place where you are... your lovely country is seen at this time that it shall break up into five islands. And the reason for this is because of the consciousness, the variety if you would, of levels of consciousness of all ones within your continent...

SOLTEC (continues) ...The tilting of the axis, if you will, and the discussion of three stages of this, is to assist in the acclimation of the alteration... But you are sitting at an angle, hmm? As you would come and this would go this way (shows axis moving clockwise)... So if you were sitting here and you have a specific climate, you may find that you have moved over here, and you have become closer to what you call your Equator, hmm? But recognize the Equator is shifting, and you are moving actually further away, if you will, from that which you call your polar regions. So you will find that you would experience a greater variety, perhaps, in temperature and weather patterns than you are experiencing now.

But now you have to add to this, you understand. What part of your planet are you speaking of? If, as we have spoken of, your country or your continent is to be divided, or will be divided because of the vibrational pattern of the entities who are in varying locations upon the planet and because of the activity of the Illuminati within your own continent, your actual geophysical appearance will be altered. There will be areas which had seemed to you to be areas which you would not inhabit that will become habitable because of the change in the tilt of the axis. There will be that which will be a balancing within those areas, and certain flora and fauna will begin to grow in those areas in order to make them more habitable for you.

Remember as you experience the changes, the geophysical changes upon the planet, there will be portions which shall sleep and there will be portions which shall rise up from their sleep. So the whole picture of planet Earth has the potential to be greatly changed.

Climates will change. Areas which had been quite cold will become more temperate. Some temperate areas will become much colder. The animal and the plant life in those areas will alter according to their own adaptability to specific areas, or there will be migration. In some instances, new animal and plant life will be introduced and in other instances animal and plant life will be re-introduced, because they have been removed that they might be more refined and have a period of rest before they return.

So you could anticipate, if all goes now according to the way that it is understood, where you are now shall be recognized as an island. And you will be in a climate which would have greater variations in temperature, because you would find you have moved closer to that which you would call your equatorial belt, recognizing that equatorial belt will change. It will not be in the same position it is now...

And New Zealand?

DIONUS Beloved ones of Earth, I am Dionus. ...When we have referred to your land to this one through which I speak, we have referred to it as the ancient land. What does this mean? Your geologists and your learned scientists will give you many explanations of how you have come with the islands which you are on. And one day they will see the truth. For you are tips of mountains.

There is a great land below you that connects your islands, for your islands are the tops of the mountains and your plains are the valleys between the mountains. You are a portion of Lemuria, the beautiful land when it was of peace and it was of harmony, as it rests now. If you had the finite instruments that you could measure, you would find your shore line is greater than it was a 100 years ago, even than it was 10 years ago. For indeed your islands are growing for you are rising up. And you who live on these mountain tops, are ones who have returned to your land, your native land. And you have come for a longing of balance, for the simplicity of being attuned with all that is about you, and the open communication with that which is beyond.

Some of you chose your parents to enter into this area at this time. Others of you have left other portions of your planet, to come to these islands, these mountain tops.

If you had the eye to see as I see, you could see where you were in Lemuria. At the time this land went beneath the waters to sleep, there were ones who gathered in this area, and there were teachings which were safely tucked within the peaks of the mountains to be brought forth in a new day. There was technology, as you would call it, which is recorded on crystalline chips. And I would suggest you do not go digging through your mountains looking for these, for you will not find them yet. But they are placed within, safe keeping, within your mountain ranges until man is ready to use the knowledge.

Some of you were involved within temples that held this knowledge in the time of Lemuria, and you were involved in bringing the crystalline bits that they would be collected in specific areas. So that is one reason why you are where you are and that tells you a little bit about the history of your island on your planet.

And then one will look up with eyes very clear and they will say, "But what is my purpose in all of this", hm? Has that crossed your mind? I thought so. For you see there was a portion of my consciousness, too, which once walked upon your plane.

You will go through in the next six months on your calendar, a rapid acceleration in your own growth process -- each of you, who desires this. You will note at the end of this period that you do not feel to be the same person that you did six months ago. This is in preparation and this is also to assist the others on your planet, on your islands, to come into a balance themselves...

Do you know what a drop-in is? It is one who comes from another dimension to work for a time within your dimension. They take on the form and all of the characteristics which you have. It is not the case of a walk-in in which the physical being is used as a vehicle by two divine portions. It is not that. These ones come in their own essence. And you have an area within your islands which we can bring ones in to acclimatize themselves to the vibrational pattern of your planet. From there they may be relocated to areas such as when you have a disaster, an earthquake, or perhaps there has been a mud slide, or perhaps one of your plane crashes, or many things which you call catastrophes -- these are then relocated that they might become active members of society, assisting brothers and sisters on the planet. But the point of entry or one of the points of entry is within your island system. Again I would strongly urge you don't go looking for it because you will not find it. I promise that from the Totality of my Being.

What about Thailand?

SOLTEC Thailand is to go through many changes, especially through the government and its peoples. These changes will have direct impact on the land itself. There shall be a dis-ease-ment which will sweep through the lands which will decrease the dense population to a proportion which is compatible with the Earth Mother in that location. Those who are outside the city densities will observe what is happening in the cities, but not be as affected by the dis-ease-ment. There shall be a land shifting in the final stages which will separate peoples causing at first confusion and hysteria, and then calm and peace. Watch the rise and fall of the waters. When the waters fall to a low, low level be advised it has begun.

The Japanese are very concerned about what is going on with Mother Earth and earthquakes so they have been

using needles that they sink into the earth, claiming that this is supposed to have a healing effect. They are trying to get these things dispersed throughout the world. Is this in fact a useful device to promote healing?

SOLTEC ...You are familiar with that which is the healing practice called acupuncture? ("Yes. That is what they are relating it to.") This is the relationship, and it is that one needle in one place will not do as much as those points which are recognized about the planet that are stimulated to assist in the healing, but it must be within the ley lines, the flow. Even as the acupuncture needles or the acupressure is used on the physical being of man, this is the same principle. You can have the same results if man will work with man in this area.

It is also advisable to use crystalline energy when this is done -- that the hollow needle itself is not sufficient but the use of the crystal with the needle would be most beneficial... You would place the crystal at the top of the needle -- and here what are we saying is top and bottom, or top and base? ("The base would be the point that you would put it into the Earth?") This is so. And the top would be that which would remain outside that is in view. For it would be then that the energies could be beamed to the crystal causing a vibration within the hollow that is the needle which will go and then vibrate on the conjunction of the ley lines, assisting...

How deep would the needle have to go?

SOLTEC I am pausing here that I would get this in relative terms. It would be considered a shaft which would be several miles, even as you have those which are shafts in which you would drill for precious metals or you would bring forth substances from the Earth. It would be of greatest benefit if it is several miles. Those which you would call ones of other countries have the concept but they have not quite refined it yet to its most useful purpose, to its most usefulness.

Could that be done also through radiothesia?

SOLTEC This can be done in this manner. However, it is a diluted way to do this because you can understand of the intensification.

How long will it take for all the changes to take place so that this planet can be a place of peace and harmony? It seems it would take thousands and thousands of years to accomplish this. Is that true?

HATONN ...I would remind you here, my dear, a thousand of your years can be as the sigh within Eternity. Ones of Earth, many ones of Earth have voiced a preoccupation with time, date, hour. Many ones have sold of their homes. They have closed of their business. They have given up their possessions. And they have gone to the hillside to wait for our arrival, believing that it shall come on the morrow. I cannot give a date. I cannot give an hour or a minute on your clock, for it is up to man and up to his choice in the upcoming days.

Yes, the cycle shall close. And the closing shall not be one that shall be a smooth transition into the next. For this has been man's choice of the past and he has sealed into that which he has chosen. But I would urge each of you, do not be concerned how long, or what it shall take. For those of you that shall return to Earth to be inhabitants of Earth in the New Day shall be prepared, shall be of an age, or I should say of a physical ability that you shall be able to do that which you have come to do.

Those of you that shall be with us shall recognize how your time limits you of Earth and your thinking processes. You have been quite locked into this thought of time, this thought of year, of day, of month, of hour, of moment, of day, of week. Your whole existence, your whole being is reflecting this thing you call time. You look to that which has happened, that which is of your history, and you must give this a day, an hour, a year. For it is necessary within your present thinking to put all in their proper dimension, their proper perspective. And this is the tool that you use.

I would say to you for a moment to remove time from your thoughts, and to see all as a chain of events. As this happens so does the next, and the next, and the next. See your spiral, if you will, that has no start. It has no finish but continually moves ever so slowly upward. One portion follows the next which follows the next. This is your cycles. There is not time. There is that one which follows the other, that does produce your cycle, that does produce your change.

During the changes it has been predicted there will be three days of darkness. Is that correct?

SARNA ...To briefly comment upon that which are your three days of darkness. There have been, to my awareness through this channel when first we began to speak with ones in circles, eight times mentioned the three days of darkness. This originally came to conscious awareness on that which was the beginning of this decade that you are finishing (1980's). Each year there surfaces that which are the three days of darkness.

Each of you has experienced your three days of darkness. What is darkness? It is the absence of Light, is it not? Have you not each had your own period in which your Light was absent?

Do not put your energy into this thinking mode, for if you do, or when you do, you are setting up barriers yourself. Put your energies into always seeing and maintaining the Light, the perfection that you are and that all is...

Can you tell us about the inner earth people, their lifestyle, looks, foods, etc.?

SARNA ...The ones that are known to you as your inner earth people are ones who initially have lived on the surface of your planet. But as the overall decay of the surface of the planet has come about they chose to go within. Their's is an atmosphere that is lighted by Divine Light. There are activities there, lifestyles that are in some ways similar to that which is on our ships. There is an open communication with those of us in this form with those that are within your earth's surface or the core of your planet. We have bases there where ships might be housed for brief periods of time.

The form is more of an etheric form than your own. These ones are quite light, are quite fair. Indeed, you would see them as ones that are white. There is an intake of foodstuffs, but it is on a much lighter scale than that which you are familiar with. These ones are more evolved along their evolutionary path than you upon the surface. They too are working to assist you in raising your vibratory rate, your conscious awareness that they might be able to openly and easily communicate with you.

There are places on the surface of your planet that are as doors or gateways to the Inner Earth. No, I would not advise any of you to make a wholesale exit to these areas, for indeed you would find them closed when you arrive.

Many ones of the Inner Earth have been evacuated in anticipation of the earth changes that are coming about. Those that are there have remained there by choice. And in some instances they shall be coming to the surface to work with you and to work with ones of your governments in assisting you to bring about a peaceful coexistence upon the surface of your planet. However, they recognize that this shall take a great deal of effort on their part. They will not come to the surface and stay for any extended period of time until it shall be safe for them to do so, and they have received the safety assurance of your government prior to doing so. There have been ones of your government that have gone within the earth's crust to talk with, to meet with the leaders, the councilors of the inner earth people...

If we took a photograph of one of the inner earth people, would they show up?

HATONN ...I doubt that one would come up to you and say, "I am from Inner Earth", and this would be something that would not be discussed in great detail. If the occasion arose that one was seen in their true form, they would not register on that which is your photographic equipment, but you would have merely a very bright place on that which would be your photograph.

Are some of those beings presently incarnated on the surface of the Earth?

HATONN ...There are ones that have taken on form on your planet. This has been for relatively brief periods, but there are no ones from the Inner Earth evolution that are in the embodiment process that you are using on the face of Mother Earth, for there is not need for this -- just as there are ones from throughout the Cosmos that walk among you, though you know them not as being any different than you are, other than they are ones with ideals that seem to you high, or they would seem to have a particular air about them. There would be a peacefulness, there would be a knowing and an understanding, a tolerance, that you would experience. And you would say, "This is one of my brothers that I would like to walk beside, that I enjoy being near."

* * * * *

It would seem that most of the questions have been answered. Some of the Fleet have already begun their return to the ships. So my dear ones, go forth in peace and joy until we return for another discussion.

Sarna out.

ADULT HU-MAN

Good evening my compatriots. We trust you have had ample opportunity to put into practice the concept of universal brotherhood. This evening as we gather, we have chosen the topic of the hu-man and its form. We will focus on the adult this meeting and next meeting will be about the child hu-man. Our speakers for this topic will be Commanders Ashtar, Emartus, Beatrix, Hatonn, Jokhym, and Monka. Captains Almeta, Alerva, Keilta and I will also share thoughts and answer questions. The first speaker is Commander Emartus.

* * * * *

Greetings and salutations. I am Emartus that would speak. For those of you that do not know me, I am a cosmic healer and I would perhaps be one that would be more tuned to the vibration of the healing process and the balancing process upon your planet...

Physically, your form is having great difficulty with the energies as they are coming in, for your form is attuned to the vibratory rate of that which is your planet. And so as the vibratory rate of the planet is being altered, so it is that the form that you are currently using must be modified also. Thus energies are being beamed to you that there is a decrease in the molecular structure within your form. You are losing your denseness. You are becoming lighter. You are becoming lighter as far as your heaviness, your weight upon your planet.

Could the infusion cause some of us to have periods of being very tired and sometimes dizzy?

EMARTUS ...It would sound like you have a problem. And indeed, you do not. What you are experiencing is a heightened sensitivity to the vibrational change within your form. Translated, you are feeling as the energies are coming into your sphere of consciousness, and as your form is changing its vibrational frequency, its vibrational pattern.

And you say to me, "That's well and good. I still feel miserable." Listen to your form and allow it to rest if it needs to rest, or to be nourished if it needs to be nourished. You have that upon your planet which is called a clock, and there seems to be a definite enslavement to this clock. Is this not so? Watch this pattern that you speak of, of the tiredness. When does it come? Is it because you have consumed a large quantity of foods, or is it because you have not consumed enough foods? Tune to, go within, and see what your form is telling you. This I would say to all ones upon the planet. You are not used to, you have forgotten how to tune to your vehicle, to see what it is that it is saying to you.

For some of you that are going through an alteration in energy patterns, you are experiencing a severe headache, a severe discomfort in your brain, in your whole housing for your thinking process. Indeed, there are those of you that would say, you would feel that your head was going to come off, there is such an intensity. Or you would desire that it would be removed, because of the intensity. In such an incidence, recognize that there is an alteration that is going on in your vibrational structure. There are those energies which are being shared with you to assist you in coming into an understanding, a knowing, awakening that sleeping portion of your brain.

Allow yourself to be in a relaxed state. Perhaps have something which is warm to drink, which is comforting to you. There are various potions upon your planet that you might take that would ease of your discomfort, and allow yourself to rest. For some it might be that you would place a moist cloth over your eyes and over your forehead, that it would give you some relaxation, some peace. Note the pattern of this discomfort, where it is, its intensity, how it lasts. In some instances, it might say to you that there is a tenseness, there is a weight that you are carrying. Is this discomfort in the shoulder area? Does it radiate up the back of your neck and around to the front of your head? Is this what happens? Are you carrying, are you tense? In such an instance, there are those about your planet that would be called masseuses, and they would assist in relaxing the muscular form of your being and would assist in the releasing of these tensions that you are experiencing.

Oft times there is that which is to be considered which is called the diet, the intake for your vehicle. Look at your intake. What are you eating? What are you consuming? And when do you consume it? There is a great desire upon your planet for all ones to eat at specific periods, particularly in that which is your country. You have what is considered three meals a day, whether you want them or not. Is this not correct? Listen to your form. Feed it when it wants to be fed, and feed it what it wants to eat.

There will be that period in which you would say, "I feel a great desire for a piece of fruit that is juicy." Well then, by all means have this. It does not mean that you must sit down at a particular time and consume a great quantity of foods. But listen to what your form needs, when it needs it, and you would find you would have much more comfort. You would have less of your up-and-down patterns, but rather you would have more of a constancy.

Intake ample, ample amounts of water. This might be in that which are called your herb teas. It might be that you would desire to drink the hot water with a little of your lemon juice and honey in it. But have ten glasses of your water each day, for this allows for the flushing of your system to release the impurities that build up merely by being in the environment that you are in, and also allows for an even flow of energies through you. For how does energy flow? It flows through the liquid systems of your being. And so it is, have your water in whatever form that would be comfortable for you.

As your vibratory rates of your vehicles are being altered according to your own desire for evolvement, you will find that certain foods, certain beverages that have been ones of great companionship to you no longer will be as comfortable as they have been. You will find as you would listen to your form that there would be those things that you were used to, per se, that no longer have an appeal. Or though you would consciously desire them, when you would intake them you would find that you would become ill or you would have a great discomfort.

May I also suggest that which has been the, shall we say, remedy that another one has put forth for you upon the planet, and that is a teaspoon of honey and a small piece of cheese when you feel a particularly low period, for this would give you a quick fix -- I believe is your term -- and it would also give you a certain sustaining quality.

But look at your dietary intake, and do not confine yourselves or limit yourselves to your three meals a day, but allow yourselves to eat, to intake, to ingest when you need to, and you will find you have greater comfort.

BEATRIX Greetings, beloveds. ...There are those of you upon your plane at this time -- and here I do not do this as a blanket thing -- that seem to be at a low frequency as far as your mineral zinc is concerned. You will find that a small portion of this each day assists you in accepting the alteration in vibrational pattern. But here you listen to your form and what it tells you if this would be of assistance to you.

That which are the cleansing baths are also of great benefit in balancing. When you would come from your place of toil or from your marketplace, cleanse your form and wash away the unbalances that you have collected. And you will find this is what you would call refreshing, but in truth it is helping to rid you of some of the unbalances and assist you in bringing about a balance within your own sanctuary which can be nourishing for you and revitalizing...

It has been said that people have been talking about feeling irregular heartbeats.

EMARTUS There are those that have done this, as there are those who have headaches, there are those who have had dizziness. This is all your interpretation and understanding of the alteration and the molecular change of your form...

There are some of you who have noted you have had a great decrease or a drop in your temperatures. There are others that have noted a change in your blood pressure. There are those of you who suddenly have become hypoglycemic, and various others unbalances have manifested as your molecular structure is adjusting to the change in vibrational pattern.

Do the sunspots affect the magnetic field in our bodies?

EMARTUS This is so. And you would think, even as you ask that question, if all things are interrelated, whatever would happen on Jupiter would affect your magnetic body, would it not, your magnetic field?...

How can I maintain a balance in the work setting?

ALMETA Good evening, my compatriots, I am that one that is known as Almeta. Some of you recognize the energy pattern that I share with you. For others of you, it might seem as a new one, as I would introduce specific energies that are my attunement and my frequency. With your permission, I shall speak briefly to offer a measure of assistance for some of the things that you each are experiencing now...

Ones have not grasped the importance, yea, the necessity of being centered before they go forth to their vocations. Those places in which most of you work, are cramped. Your air ventilation is inadequate. There are many ones about that would be as chimneys puffing smoke away which clouds the air for all ones. And here, this is choice. You are required by your social standing, by your own peer groups to be dressed in a particular manner for a particular vocation.

And so you go forth to these places of employment, usually having your being filled with those foods that have a high degree or high concentration of sugar in them -- and these are refined sugars. You have dashed, you have hurried. Indeed, along your route you have inhaled the fumes from other autos. You enter into a building with minimal windows, so you have no exposure, visually or otherwise to your out of doors. And you are expected to sit in a cramped position with clothing that is not particularly comfortable, but is quite binding, and at best be productive and creative. Is this not accurate?

Now, may I offer this for your suggestion. Even though most of you on planet Earth would stay in your beds till the very last second, you are allowed the freedom of doing so. However, as you lay in your bed, center yourself in the Light. Feel it's enfoldment as it surrounds you and be the peace and tranquility that is now yours to enjoy. This shall come gradually to you as you practice this. Feel a delicious moment of attunement as you lie within your bed or you sit in a comfortable chair and you are at peace with all that is about you. Indeed, you and your bed or your chair are one. Feel this joy and this peace. This is the first thing that you must do, is be centered and balanced before you go forth.

Then may I suggest that you partake of the natural fruits and vegetables. If you would have that which is called your toasted "wafers", may I suggest your whole grain ones. And yes, your milk, for this will give you a staying power that your physical vehicle needs at this point within your evolution. Then allow yourself to dress in clothing that would be acceptable but that does not constrict. Allow yourself to have room to breathe easily and to be flexible.

For those of you that enter the work place and you have no contact with Mother Nature, may I suggest that you have a picture, either on your wall or perhaps on your desk -- a small one that would be a scene of nature that is most pleasing and most relaxing for you. At this point, I would not advise or suggest that you petition your employers to cut holes in your walls, but initially use this picture as a means to assist you in attuning with Mother Nature. Of course this may be changed with your seasons and as your needs vary.

Now those periods within your day that are known as your breaks for nourishment, may I suggest that you go out of doors. It would be advantageous for you to take of your nourishment out of doors, but if this is not possible, to just walk briefly. This would assist you.

Oh, may I add another thought for your consideration. As we spoke of the picture or the landscape, some of you might find a great satisfaction in having a plant, a green plant on your desk or in your room. For this will give you increased clean, clear oxygen as well as being most pleasing to the eye.

But to return. At your time of repast, I would offer that you consider going out of doors -- if at all possible to get your feet off of pavement or man made gravel or such, but be able to walk upon the grass or the soil of Earth for a few moments. This will assist you in balancing those unresolved energies that might have entered your field since you entered your place of employment.

You will find that this is quite relaxing. And indeed, you might verbally say, "I release these unresolved energies to Mother Earth that she would use them in balance and harmony." I would suggest that as you do this that you might find, indeed, a relaxation. You might find this as a most peaceful way for spending this midday period.

Again at those periods which are known on Earth as your coffee break times, I offer for your consideration that you might want to partake lightly of fruits or fruit juices, and perhaps a small piece of cheese. This will give you a balance and a stability so that you have a constant energy flow within your being. This too will also assist you in maintaining a more even balance within yourself.

And then as you would leave of your place of employment, I would suggest that you release those thoughts that have been with you that they would not cloud your field as you enter of your vehicles to return to your dwellings.

Once you have returned to your dwelling, may I again suggest that you take off the clothing that you were wearing, for these have accumulated specific energies and specific thought forms with them, and put that clothing on which is comfortable, which is most pleasing to you.

Here again, I would suggest that you have a period that you might go forth that you would be in direct contact with Mother Earth -- be it the grass, be it the soil, be it the plants -- that again those unresolved energies that have come to you might go forth to Mother Earth.

In addition this will be an opportunity for any of you that have been in a modified atmosphere to again feel of the balance and to breathe deeply of the fresh, clean air that is so abundant at this particular period upon your Earth. After this you might again partake of those foods which are nourishing and satisfying to you without weighing you down or causing a heaviness.

During that period that is known as your period of relaxation before you retire to slumber, may I suggest that you enter again into a period of meditation, a period of balancing and attunement so that as you prepare for slumber, you are truly at peace and at one. Thus your body might recharge and regenerate during its sleep period, so that this period would be a most advantageous one for you...

Would you talk to us about disease and the human body?

EMARTUS ...That which is known to you upon your planet as dis-easement is created by an energy unbalance. This unbalance can be within the individual. Or, there are those of you upon your planet that collect the energy patterns of others and manifest these in an unbalanced state, thus causing a dis-easement within the individual. When you, upon your planet, are not of a balanced state, may I suggest to you that:

    1) You look at your own state, you evaluate where you are and why you are not in balance; what has brought about your dis-easement, and then take steps to rectify this. In some instances, as you would evaluate your individual position you become aware that you are feeling or you are experiencing a dis-easement that is one attributed to the overall evolutionary status of those that are about you. Thus you are reacting to the energy flow of other ones that are not in a state of balance and harmony, thus creating an unbalance within you. In such an instance, may I suggest that you would seek the assistance of ones that are in balance to help to bring about your own balance.

    2) There are many patterns that are being played through at this time upon your planet. Great energies are going into healing and assisting ones in the healing process. I would caution you to always remember that one does not heal another but it is that you might be a facilitator to assist in bringing about an energy flow that might be used or utilized for the highest good of the one that is not in balance.

    I will illustrate this last particular point for you. As ones of the Fleet have entered into that which is a lower vibratory frequency, they have experienced a reaction to this frequency and much of the negativity that is held within the frequency. Thus, they have experienced loss of limb, or dismemberment, or withering in some instances. As they would again enter into the vibrational frequency that was their natural one for their particular manifestation, they have found that they do not have a complete form because of their reaction to the lower vibratory frequencies. In this instance, we, the cosmic healers, would come together to assist this one in holding the Divine Thought that they might again manifest the limb that would be missing or to bring about an easement or a balancing within their form. Our energies are but facilitators to assist this one as we, with them, would hold the Divine Thought of Perfection that they are.

There are the two primary reasons that I have stated for your periods of dis-easement. In addition, may I bring one more thought for your consideration. As energy patterns are introduced to the planet and to ones of the planet, the form that you are using is not accustomed to these particular energy patterns. For indeed, the form is more accustomed to a vibratory frequency that is less finely attuned. Thus it reacts to these energies, for the energy patterns are creating an unbalance within the cellular structure of the vehicle. As the vehicle becomes accustomed to the energy patterns, so it is it is allowed the opportunity to adjust, and there comes about a harmony between the energy patterns and the vehicle.

So there are several possibilities for your states of dis-easement. And I have not mentioned those that have been brought about by embodiment karma, or those dis-easements that are used as cleansing processes for your planet, or those that are the thought forms that have been manifest by you upon your planet. But I have merely mentioned those that have been brought about as a reaction to specific energy patterns.

Did I understand correctly that limbs could be made to grow back?

EMARTUS ...Indeed, you have this capability and this potential. However, the manifestation of this in toto is not yet available to you at your present vibrational pattern. This opportunity, this ability has always been within you. But as you have reduced your vibratory frequency you have also reduced your ability to bring about these manifestations. You have accepted your particular vibratory pattern with a minimal desire or initiative on your part to go beyond that which is known to you now. Recognize I do not speak to you as the individual, rather I am speaking to man collectively upon the planet.

As your vibratory rate is elevated and your energy pattern is increased, you will be able to come together to create a specific pattern in order to manifest missing limbs, or perhaps to heal dis-eased organs, or in such instances that you might have a broken bone, to be able to bring this into an alignment and a state of perfection. Indeed, this gift, as you would call it, is not one that is far removed from you, but is one that is easily within your grasp.

There are a number of diseases that are becoming more prevalent and new ones that are cropping up. Is there any relationship between these new diseases that are showing themselves and the changes that are coming about as far as the evolutionary cycle is concerned? Are there certain diseases that are related to certain people and certain abilities?

EMARTUS ...May I suggest to each of you that you look at these conditions that are about your planet. What has brought them into manifestation? What consciousness has brought them into manifestation? For indeed, what is your disease called cancer? It is a collection. It is a self-destructive collection of thought forms that have manifested.

There are those conditions, diseases, if you will, about your planet that are serving a great purpose, for indeed, they are giving opportunity as cleansing tools. And there are ones about your planet that would select to no longer function upon your planet and they have chosen to terminate their physical being in this manner. There are others that are taking on specific attributes, shall we say, of the collective consciousness -- shall we call them negative attributes -- shall that be a contradiction in your terms -- and as they have done this, they are doing so to help the karmic pattern of the collective consciousness of your planet to be lessened, to decrease.

So, there is a two-fold manner in which these conditions are being brought about, and each one's involvement is as individual and unique as is their own soul pattern. There is no particular disease or condition that is more manifested in those with gifted abilities or psychic abilities than there are those that do not. For indeed, it is a choice of the soul prior to the entrance into the physical form for this particular embodiment as to what conditions, etc., that they would be involved in, or what experience they would have.

May I also add the thought that as there are the offshoots of various diseases, such as that which is your disease that is known to you as AIDS; some of your cancerous conditions; some of your genetic conditions, these are a direct result of the level or the thinking or the external manifestation of the thought forms of the collective consciousness in its present state. So, even though the collective consciousness would bring forth specific conditions, these are tools that are used for the over-all upliftment and evolvement process upon the planet.

Each one, each man -- and I use that term to include both the male and the female -- each one has the ability to heal themselves. This is an art that has long since been forgotten or ignored through the various build-ups and the convenience of various potions and their availability upon your planet. So therefore, the ability to heal oneself has not been used, shall we say, in recent evolutionary cycles upon your planet, but it has been minimized. And this gift, or this activity, has been left up to others to do for you.

You mentioned that some of the people that come down with these particular diseases are balancing out some of the karma for the planet. Why isn't scientific research bringing about cures for these particular diseases? Is it because of the balancing effect that could be brought about?

EMARTUS That which is your medical profession are ones that look for cures. They look for potions and they look for various remedies that might be done to another. The answer for all conditions lies within the individual and their own active involvement and their desire for cure.

You must also recognize there are many ones upon your planet who are ill, who have various illnesses, and they do not desire to be cured. For it is, they would lose their identity if they were cured. For there are those that have great gifts, and as I have said, each has the ability to cure themselves. And this is not that which would be taken lightly, for truly you have this gift. But most ones, when you would get to an analysis find that they do not want to be cured, for the illness helps them to maintain an identity in some instances.

So, you must first look at why an individual has a particular condition. Is it, and again I shall emphasize it is as variable as there are individuals upon your planet, for it may be for the karmic, to help to absolve part of the karma for the collective consciousness. It might be an individual acceptance in order to further their own evolution. It might be that which is a reaction to an experience upon the planet and they have accepted this condition, they have desired it, they have manifested it in order to bring about a particular experience for themselves, or for others.

So, these are but three brief examples, and there would be as many examples as there are beings upon the planet, for each one is unique and it would be that you must look at the individual as to why they are involved in this particular condition...

How can we turn the tide as far as the disease AIDS is concerned?

EMARTUS ...First, shall we look at that which was the origin of this condition. The origin of this condition was the misuse of that which were Creator energies. And, just as has happened in past situations upon Earth plane, there have been those that have become involved that were innocently involved.

There are ones upon your planet that have been given specific formulas that would terminate this condition. Indeed, many of you shall be hearing of this shortly.

This condition that has received such wide and varied acclaim upon your planet is one that is not new, is not one that has just sprung up within your last decade, but rather, it is a condition that has been with you upon the planet for well over 100 years. But it has not been diagnosed by your physicians until most recently.

Man is quick to judge man. Man is quick to judge that which he considers not acceptable to his own particular manner and mode. This particular condition is a manifestation that is twofold. Misuse of Creator energies as well as prejudgment. Prejudgment, or judgment, has accelerated this condition. As man can look upon man as equal, as brother, so shall it be that this condition shall begin to decrease upon your planet.

As I stated earlier, the cure, if this would be the term you would select to use, has been given to ones upon your planet, and indeed, this cure shall become available to the masses in your near future. Love, acceptance, brotherhood. These are the primary criteria for bringing about the decrease in this condition, as well as those other ones about your planet that are used to remove life forms before they have lived their extended period.

For those that have drug and alcohol problems, is there an etheric webbing that becomes damaged?

HATONN Greetings, dear ones. This is a most interesting question. This etheric webbing that you speak of are the lines, strings, rays, call these what you will, that come forth to ones on planet Earth. These nourish the etheric being. An example would be one on your plane that has chosen the path of alcohol, of drink. Here I speak of one that is consumed, on your earthly terms would be considered an alcoholic. This, because this sets up a non-positive terminal as the rays come in to the individual, indeed, it damages, it repels the healing, nourishing energies that come to feed the physical being as well as the etheric one.

Now, to continue with our example. This one that has been consumed by drink is also one that is quite easily used by ones in your astral planes that have not released themselves from Earth. Indeed, theirs is a vicarious enjoyment through this one that is consumed by his habit of drinking. But should this one choose that this is not the path that they would walk, that they would no longer be ruled by their alcohol consumption, then the energies that have come forth to nourish this individual -- and here I speak of all the bodies of this individual -- are made stronger. The terminal is one that is conducive to receiving the energies. There is a lightening and a strengthening of the waves that come to the individual.

Nothing is ever lost, should one lift up their voice to reclaim their inheritance, their right. This, ones on Earth must understand. They are not lost. No one is lost unless they choose not to lift up their thoughts for a uniting with their Divine Principle.

What are your thoughts concerning the many organ transplants that are being done at this time?

JOKHYM Salutations, my brothers and sisters of planet

Earth. ...When man came to Earth -- and here I speak of the soul of man as he enters the babe -- the veil does fall. And for most ones that walk about your Earth they have no recollection of their yesterdays or of that which might be their tomorrows. They see only this moment -- and by this I mean this particular lifetime. Consequently, they would not leave of this lifetime, for they see this as all there is or ever will be. Oh yes, they spout and they regurgitate the teachings of life after death. And they see these winged angels that fly about with harps and trumpets. But this is an unreality to them. The reality is the physical being that they have at this moment. And most ones are not ready to leave of this physical vehicle.

Now as I say this and I have shared this lesson with you I must also qualify my statement. For here again as each soul is a separate entity unto itself and its path is unique to its own, so are its steps in any given embodiment. Man by his various transplants -- and many of your physicians will recognize this in the future days -- is merely trying to do that which he has done in ages past. For in those life times there was no death as Earth man knows it now. There was merely the laying aside of one vehicle to enter another to go forth. So it is man does not recognize this. However, depending on the journey of the particular soul in some instances these transplants, these exchanges, this sharing of ones being with another has had a greater significance and impact than is realized on your physical plane. For as one gives of his portion, a portion of his life stream to sustain another so is this one of the supreme acts of service, for in this both have the opportunity to finish that which they have come to do...

If we have chosen, prior to embodiment, a certain life pattern for evolvement, and this pattern is interrupted by a premature death, what happens? Do we plan this?

SARNA This question that you ask, the only response I can give you is one that it is a very individual situation. In most instances, those who leave their life form in an abrupt manner do not plan to do so, but they are given opportunity of re-embodiment again. Now, just because a form, a soul, would leave their embodiment abruptly, does not mean that they would be bound to Earth, for this again would be an individualized state. There are those that have lived their full lifetime, if you would, upon your planet and they still do not choose to leave the planet. But rather, as you would say, they hang around because they like it there and they will not accept the thought that they are not in embodiment.

So those that have left their form abruptly do not necessarily remain Earth bound. There are those ones on the other side that are of the angelic kingdom that work with those that leave their form abruptly. Those that would choose to hang around Earth, as you would say, are ones that will not accept the help that is offered to them. In such an instance, they are allowed to stay until they are willing to go toward the Light of Creator Source.

You, upon your planet, may assist these ones in their journey. Those of you that would have communication, encourage these ones to go to the Light. Encourage them to look about for ones that would offer them assistance, for they are there. Do not encourage them to stay with you upon the planet.

Much of your grieving process is one that pulls departed souls close to the Earth plane. This is a most unfortunate situation for you will not allow these ones to be free to go on their journey, but rather, you would pull them back and slow their progression down. You, as a thinking entity, have the responsibility of assisting these ones. If they have been in an accident or they have changed dimensions abruptly, oft times they might be confused and not recognize where they are. By your assistance, they can go with ones who are waiting for them to assist them in walking into the Light, that they might be allowed a period of rest, of balancing and recuperation, before they are again presented with lessons and further steps in evolvement, for they would be allowed their healing process. You who would mourn excessively for those that have left your dimension are doing them a great disservice, for you are binding them close to your plane and not allowing them to go forth.

I trust this has answered your question and has also planted a seed that each of you might ponder in your quiet moments.

MONKA I greet you in the Light of the Source. ...[Regarding those] whose life is terminated abruptly by the act of another, and this was not selected by them prior to embodiment -- in such an instance, the divine portion, the soul is removed just prior to the ceasing of the life breath that they might come into a state of Light. Though, this is an individual process that cannot be given as one sentence would cover all situations, for indeed, each situation is unique unto the particular individual that is involved.

What about our thought patterns? Do they have impact on things outside of us?

MONKA ...Let us think and let us talk about your thoughts. You upon your planet have felt this was one area of your being that defied intrusion. Then as you have grown along your path you have become aware that your thoughts are your abilities to manifest. And indeed, much of the clouding, the muddying of the waters so to speak, have been the result of the thought forms, the unfinished thought forms that have been projected by ones upon your planet. Indeed, your thoughts have been the contributing factor to the storm clouds over much of your sphere.

What do you think? What do you think, O'brother of Earth? Think of that for a moment. Is there perfection within your thoughts? Is there manifestation of your godliness? Is there only Divine Light manifest from that which you think?

What would you create with your thought? What is your perfection? What is your perfection?

For those that have the gift of sight beyond the physical range there are great unfinished thought forms that hover about the planet. This is a period in which you have opportunity to manifest your thoughts. When your anger would be piqued by your spouse or perhaps a fellow worker and you would think unbalanced thoughts, is this what you would manifest for them? For recognize with the Law of Cause and Effect that as you project unfinished thought forms, so it is that these of like energy patterns will return to you. Yes, of like energy patterns! As these particular energies are allowed to enter the ethers of Earth, you shall experience your thought forms returning to you much more quickly than you have in the past. You have been urged to guard well the words that would come from your mouths. You have been urged to temper your actions, and to think of these.

And now, I say to you beloved ones, shall we take the next step? Shall we work upon that which we think so that which we do and which we feel and which we say would be in even a more perfect state?

Project only that which is the perfection. As thoughts that are not of balance, that are not of harmony would come to you, release these quickly and ask that they would be returned to Divine Source to come forth in perfection. Do not hold on to them for this merely assists them in their own growth. But allow them to go forth to Source to return in perfection. Acknowledge that which you do that is not of your highest good and your highest order, and release it that you might attain your highest good of your highest order.

As we grow in our awareness and we recognize that we are thinking thoughts of a lower vibrational pattern can they be cancelled or balanced?

MONKA ...Such wisdom there is in the question, for it shows a decided growth. At the present state where you are you have not sufficiently mastered control of all of your thoughts, but to be aware that you have not mastered this control, is indeed, a great step in your own evolvement and enlightenment. May I offer for your suggestion that as you have thoughts that you consciously know are of a lower vibratory rate that you might enfold these in love. And as you enfold them in love which is the Divine Love, so are they elevated and so then can you release them into the Cosmos that they might be balanced, that they might be neutralized.

Release these thoughts. Enfold them as you release them, and then do not dwell on them that you would add energy to them but leave them at the energy that they were as they came forth from you originally. As you do this so shall you become more and more aware of your thoughts, and so shall you become more and more capable of entertaining only those thoughts which are of a higher vibratory frequency.

What is the subconscious, and what is its purpose?

JOKHYM ...You of Earth have entered into this area that you would call psychology, which is the study of your mind. There are others that would study of the body, and they would call this anatomy. There are others that would study of this and that, and they would have a name for each. And I must say I watch this with great amusement. For Earth man will not find the key to his identity until he recognizes that he is a total entity, and each is interrelated with the other. Each cell of his being has a memory. And yes, he has a memory in total, just as he has thoughts.

Now you have asked of this level called your subconscious. Let us speak for a moment. You have your conscious level do you not? This is that which you are doing at the moment and you know you are doing it. Within this conscious level you have your automatic reactions, and you have those which you perform with thought. For instance, you are not consciously aware, you are not consciously sending forth the thought that you would digest the foods which you have taken in but this is done. This is a thought process that goes forth, but you are not consciously aware of it all the time. However, you are consciously aware of the thoughts that you use as you drive your cars, as you walk down your streets, as you select your clothing, and all of the various activities that you have in this period that you call a lifetime.

Now within you is also a memory. You have a memory that goes back into that which happened from the time that you entered into this embodiment to your time of consciousness of this moment. You of Earth have dubbed this a subconscious, and might I suggest that this would be because this is just below your surface.

...May we use a pictorial illustration. If you would visualize a sheet of paper. Now across this sheet of paper draw a line. Indeed, perhaps use the bottom half of this paper, and draw your line half way across in the middle (of the full page). Now half way through (the bottom half) draw another line, and color in this portion whatever color suits your fancy. This is your conscious portion. This is that which you have recall of right now.

Below this -- and we shall color this bottom fourth of your page a mixed up gray -- this would be the portion that might be termed, in your words, your subconscious. For indeed it does operate in shades of gray.

Now notice we have one-half of our page that has no color upon it, that has no lines. Shall we call this the supra, and with your permission I shall spell this, S-U-P-R-A, supra, that which is much greater than super -- supra-conscious. For this is the total consciousness of all, and within you you have this total consciousness of all. Now within this there is the consciousness of Earth man in total that you have available to you. There is the consciousness of creation. There is the consciousness of the communion with all of us, with those that are of the higher dimensions, with the Godhead. There is also that communion which is with all that is creation. This is available to you within your supra-consciousness.

Now you of Earth, and here I speak of those that would study of your mind, have become most interested in this thing that you would call your subconscious. For this delves into those hidden things, hidden in that they are not readily available to your conscious level, that they would come forth and would help you to understand why you are reacting the way you are at this particular time. But you must recognize that this particular study is based upon this life time solely. So consequently its basis is erroneous, for your actions, your conscious actions are based upon the totality of what you are. That is heavy is it not. Yes, it is based upon the totality of that which you are, and though you would delve back into those periods of your life, this embodiment that are not easily called to your conscious level, and you would put meaning to these, this is but a part, a small portion, of that which you are. For the supra-conscious includes your present conscious thought, all that you have ever been, and all that you ever will be. And this is available to you.

Is this not a most delightful concept? Is this not most joyful to anticipate? And with this thought with you, why would you want to go into shades of gray when you have all of the rainbow to explore?

What is the function of sleep?

HATONN Your state of sleep, your state of blissful unconsciousness that each of you look forward to at the close of your day has many purposes. This is a time for your physical being to rest, to recharge, to rebuild. This is a time that you expend a minimum of physical energies. This is also the time that your spirit can come forth that you might receive of higher lessons, that you might go forth to other places within the Cosmos to learn lessons, that you might go forth to other places, to other stars, to other galaxies or to other places upon your own star to minister to others. This is an opportunity because your minds have become so strong within these physical beings, sleep is an opportunity for your spirit to be free to come forth.

At one time in your evolvement this was easily accomplished, and it was that you would hang up your physical garment that your spirit might be free to travel of the ethers. But as the physical being has grown in denseness, because of the ethers around Earth, this gift has been lost. And so your time of sleep, your time of deep meditation is a time that your spirit is freed to come forth.

So yes, sleep has many purposes for it is a renewal time for your physical being as well as your spirit. And many of the experiences that you have, that you call dreams are in actuality, those things that have happened on another dimension.

Are many of us out of body during the night on a mission?

HATONN Each of you as you sleep, as your being lies in repose, is usually out of body for at least three to four of the six to eight hours that you sleep. Each of you spends a time of ministry. And in some areas you are known as night workers or night ministers. Each of you spends a portion of time in this role; however, before you can go forth and you can minister, you must receive your own lessons, your own guidance, your own purpose. And then in small groups you go forth. And you go forth with a ministering angel, and at times at least one other.

There are always three that go forth together in spirit. And these two that are from the angelic realms see that your spirit returns to its physical being so that your physical being might be balanced and in harmony.

I might add a thought here. There are ones of you --
and I'm sure this is so of each of you -- that have said as you
have arisen in the morning, "I do not feel that my head has
touched the pillow and yet I have no recollection of being
awake." You dear ones, have been most busy during this
period of time and indeed this has been a time, a prolonged
period when your spirit has been gone from your physical
being, and this is the reason that you feel a tiredness, that
you feel a weariness is because your triune parts have been
separated for an extended period, and your spirit is weary.

**Does God speak to us in dreams to tell us what or who
we are, and how we might serve Him better?**

MONKA ...That One which you know as the Father-Mother
God, that One which you see as your Divine Creator, your
Perfect Principle speaks to each one, you and I, speaks to
each one of each planet of each place of each dimension in
all ways. Those that are attuned, that have reached an attunement know of this Divine Guidance that they receive and
know from whence it comes.

You of Earth of these eons have been content to read
in your holy word that ones spoke with God or God spoke
with ones. But you have great difficulty in recognizing that
this can happen this day on your Earth, for it does. Each one
of you each day is in constant communion with you Creator
for you are of your Creator. You are of the Perfect Principle.

O'ones of Earth, I would ask for each of you that you
might have the comfort in speaking with your Father-Mother
God that we enjoy. Yes, your Creator speaks to you in any
way, in all ways, that it might be possible for you to hear, for
you to see, for you to know. It is truly the blest that recognize
what they are receiving, and offer up their thanksgiving for
this.

Can dreams be a communication from the Masters?

SARNA Dreams are a communication with you. You are communicating with you in specific ways for you to begin to understand and accept portions of you. Oft times you will block as individuals, thoughts, knowledge, identities that you are from your consciousness. And so it is then that these come forth to assist you, to let you know you are greater than the mere limitation you have accepted.

There are those of you that would have dreams that would be prophecy. ...And here you must define that which is dream and that which is experience in spirit, for there is a difference you understand. Communication you would have with Masters would be that perhaps which is experiences while in spirit, while the form is in sleep state. But initially your dreams are for you to help you to grow within yourself. For some the dreams then become prophecy that they might foresee that which is happening with other ones...

Oft times recognize your dreams are always given to you in symbols, where your experiences in spirit shall we say, are more clearly defined, if that would help you.

An illustration would be, you might see in your dream state someone would give you a particular gemstone or flower. Now you can interpret that as an engagement ring if that particular individual has an attraction for you, or whatever. But it might be that you are trying to tell you, you have a connection with a specific Master. In your experience in spirit state you would be aware of the experience with the Master. Do you see the difference? This might help you to understand what you were doing.

Some of you are very muchly aware when your form is in sleep state you will see a ship. You will perhaps recognize a room, you will awaken to know that you have been in meetings. These are not dreams. These are you working in your spirit.

Could you talk to us about the role of the ego?

SARNA ...The ego was given to Earth man as a protector. When Earth man first entered into the dense state that he is in there were rocks, there was that which was fire, there was that which was water. Spirit experienced that it had not experienced in that vibration before. How would it know that the form that it is in would bleed if it were to cut its foot and the bleeding would result in the loss of the form? How would spirit know this? So it was given an ego.

The ego would say, "I will not place my foot there, it hurts; I will withdraw it. No, I will not step out from the cliff because in this form, my form would perish." The ego was given as a protector for your denseness within your dimension. A protector. But it is with all things, it has gotten overzealous in its protection and no longer must you be as one that is protected from walking forth from the cliff... And the ego takes such good care of you it would completely enfold you and place you as number one, and you cannot be that way.

So it is merely you would take this part of your totality and you would say, "Thank you for all the help and all the protection that you would give to me but I am my divinity and I will let that divinity guide my steps."...

When we feel anger coming on can we ask the Father to encapsulate it in Light so that it might be dissipated and not manifest itself?

MONKA Yes, by all means my brother. As you feel anger, as you feel frustration coming to you, enfold this in the golden Light of the Christed One, and release it to the Divine Creator that it might go forth to be balanced, that it might come forth to return to you in harmony and attunement.

I am well aware that you dear ones have worked most diligently in controlling your words, in attempting to control

103

your thoughts. And at this hour I would offer encouragement that you continue in your endeavors. For it is known that this is not an easy thing for you to do, just because of where you at this point in the cycle. But I would assure you that the dividends are well worth the effort. Continue in your endeavors, and we shall continue to assist you, as well as the ones of the angelic realms.

And what about fear?

JOKHYM ...Oft times when ones would express a great fear, what do they do? What is the energy that happens? They send out an energy to that which they fear, do they not? And what does that do but draw that to them? So if you have no need to bring about fear then you have no need to be concerned. If you ask each of your waking days only that will come to you for your highest good and for your highest evolvement so it is those are the experiences that will come to you and you do not have to be concerned of others. For you would not draw them to you. You would only draw that to you that would assist you. That is a universal law also though it is one that is not spoken of in great detail.

But may I use this opportunity to speak to all ones concerning that which is fear. Fear brings about an immobilization for it sets up a state of inertia, no movement. It is in that state of no movement that there can be no growth and there can be no exchange. For fear sets up the energy field that you are in a state of inertia in which there can be no exchange and that field cannot be penetrated by others.

You have that which is called adrenalin within your physical form that comes to you when you are frightened or you are put in a situation that would cause you undue distress. You are familiar with this? See this adrenalin as an immobilizer. For when you have entered into the state of fear it alters your energy pattern and stops all movement and creates a barrier for any flow. It is only as the adrenalin level decreases within you that a flow has been established.

I would bring this to your awareness for you to observe your society. Seventy-five to eighty-five percent of your
society run on adrenalin. They constantly are looking for that
which is an accelerator for them. And yet they are alone,
they are unhappy, they feel isolated, there is no interchange,
and this is shown by your number of parties where ones go
and they would say, "I was quite lonely", or the need to have
all of these possessions and wealth to prove to everyone how
prosperous they are. And yet they have driven themselves
and activated the adrenalin flow to such a point they have
placed themselves in total isolation. So what does that do?
That creates many islands that would be called your social
consciousness or your society and minimizes the interaction.

We have repeatedly said to you to have no fear.
Ones would be desired, would desire to be beamed aboard
the ships. And we have said to you to have no fear because
we cannot penetrate your field if you are in a state of fear.
But what are most ones in your society doing? They are
isolating themselves and setting up a barrier that cannot be
penetrated. They have decreased the flow. Indeed, some of
them have reached the state that they have completely shut
the flow down to a trickle -- I believe that is your word, is it not
-- to a minute dropage. For they would not allow themselves
to be in a state of a minimum of adrenalin use but rather they
have pushed themselves and they have lived their existence
with that isolated flow that they have accepted this as their
reality...

For can you see that these ones as they would continue in this manner have set up a state of isolation and of
that which you would call doom? For indeed how can they
grow or evolve and how can there be any interaction, one
with the other? For this state is observed not only in the in-
terpersonal relationships of one with the other but it is seen in
family units, that which is the key unit for the betterment of
your whole society.

Fear is an interesting mechanism that you have upon your plane. It is our desire for you that you would get past this state that you could come into more of a balance so that there would be a flow within you to assist you in your own growth.

ASHTAR With your permission I will join with you for a few moments that I might share, that our energies might mingle and intertwine. I would speak with you at this time concerning fear and the necessity in the days that lie before you, for you -- each of you of the Light -- to release all fear, and to remain calm, to be relaxed and to be centered within the Divine Christ Light.

From our vantage view we are able to see beyond your horizon and that which awaits you. Each of you shall be in for periods of great testing, of great tribulation. And, oh yes, our ones of the Dark Forces shall be ever busy causing disruption and confusion where they are allowed to enter. As the countdown approaches I cannot overemphasize the need for balance, for relaxation, for the absolute absence of fear, anxiety, or otherwise an elevated or heightened emotional state.

Each of you on the earthly plane must in the short period that is remaining learn to control your emotions. You must learn to not be governed by these. As we observe many of you, your emotional state is as the horse that runs wild and chooses not to hear the commands of its master. My dear compatriots, it is time that this wild horse be brought to rein, that it learns to walk with the other horses, that it learns to follow the commands and the directions of its master, for its own safety as well as the safety of others. In the days to come each of you shall have the responsibility of taming and controlling your own horse. I wish you well. And I add that it is vital at this hour that you succeed. You must have calmness, and there must be balance and the absence of fear within each of you. For when we come your fear vibrations shall inhibit our lifting you. Yes, dear ones, you heard me correctly. Your fear vibrations, those energies that you put forth when you are in a frightened state shall keep us from lifting you. For these vibrations are totally incompatible with our frequencies.

I realize that my words may seem quite strong to many of you, and I assure you this is for purpose for we are endeavoring, just as you are, to assist you and to assist all of mankind on Earth. But in the final hours of the final countdown we cannot bring you with us if your vibrational frequency is antagonistic to ours. I bring this to your attention at this hour that you might make an earnest effort to remove fear from your emotional vocabulary, that you might bring this wild horse to rein, that you might be as one truly to be the absolute calm that is the eye of the storm. As you do this not only shall we be able to lift you but we shall be able to work with you and through you, and to give you assistance. And to give assistance through you that might well be needed by those about you.

I speak not as a prophet-of-doom. I merely bring this to your attention that you too might grow in the Christ Light. For as you walk in the Christ Light truly there is no need for fear, there is no need for unbalance. For you truly then are one with all of creation. Thank you for allowing me these moments. I shall at this time close. I am a most humble servant of the Radiant One. And I serve with all of you to help Terra assume her place in the Confederation of the Universe.

Will you talk to us about relationships?

ALERVA Salutations, ones on planet Earth. It is my joy and my privilege to speak with you, to share energies with you, and to feel that I am a part of your circle...

I have forgotten in my evolutionary process -- indeed, to be quite truthful, I have not experienced all the experiences that you upon your planet have experienced for my mode of evolution has been a different one -- I have been of an evolutionary pattern that has been a more peaceful evolution than yours has. For you see, I have not had to experience the tribulation that many of you have had to experience. The relationships upon our planet have been most harmonious ones with a recognition in the equality of all ones. And within that recognition has been the factor of allowing each to achieve their highest potential within a specific embodiment. As I have observed you on your planet, and I have listened to those of the Fleet that have been quite close with you, I am understanding some of the experiences that you are having.

My voice, my message is primarily to those of you that are called the Legion of Volunteers. You have entered embodiment upon this planet -- and I recognize many of you, this is not your first embodiment -- but as you have taken on this particular embodiment, you have agreed to certain stipulations within your contract. However, all ones upon the planet have not agreed to the same stipulations or the same contracts. As energies are introduced into your ethers and are felt by ones upon the planet, I am sure, if you would look in retrospect, that you would note a change in relationships. Those of you who are our volunteers have welcomed this introduction of various energies. You have felt these. And though you have initially felt a measure of slight unbalance, you have quickly attuned yourselves to this energies, and your frequency has been elevated. But how has this affected your relationships? For as you would look, I am sure you will note that it has had an impact.

Have any of you experienced walking into a room or attending a meeting or a social gathering with ones, to find that others welcome you as they would a highly communicable disease? Indeed, it is as if you repulse all ones that are in your vicinity. And you are saying to yourselves, and you are looking about, and you are seeking counsel, and you are saying, "What is going on within me?" In truth dear one, you are operating at a much different frequency from these ones. And opposites do not always attract. In some cases they repel just as your magnets do. And so what happens? The energy pattern that you introduce into this particular gathering is about as welcomed as the communicable disease would be.

In other instances, are you finding that ones that you have no knowledge of, other than a casual greeting, suddenly you are developing a very close and warm relationship with these ones? And you are finding you have many wonderful things to share with them. Or are you perchance meeting someone that you know nothing of upon your plane, and finding that you have a great bond and you don't understand why? But there is an unexpressed communication between you that is understanding, that is tolerant. Or are you in a situation, relationship-wise, where you have had a comfortable relationship with one to find suddenly you are at a great unbalance? And if you would say, "Good morning", the other would say, "No, its night". Thus there is no common ground that you could reach, such as agreeing that it was high noon.

I am pointing out these obvious relationship patterns to you to spark an awareness within you, because you are not the same as you were a year ago. You are not the same as you were six months ago or three. For as energies have been allowed to enter the ethers of Earth, and indeed, specific energies have been beamed to specific ones on your planet, the vibratory frequency within the individual has been altered. Some of you have even so much as experienced implants -- crystal implants in your etheric bodies -- to assist in your own tuning mechanisms, to assist also in allowing you to be energy storers and energy carriers. We watch and we observe as relationships are changing.

Yes, your patterns of relationships are changing. Some of you that have felt a great bond and a great familial obligation are now looking at those obligations and saying, "Why do I have them?" "This parent has raised me." Or "I have raised this child." And it is now, that each is considered an adult upon your planet and is of an age of accountability when they might enter into a relationship of equality.

And there are those that are beginning to have or have begun to have communication with other dimensions. Recognizing that if you are in a relationship with another one that is not tuned to your frequency, and you begin this communion with the other dimension, this could create a rather awkward setting, could it not? Indeed, there are some that have sufficiently gotten out of balance that they have entered into brief periods of hospitalization.

I bring all of these examples to your awareness so that you might have a knowing of what is going on. Your vibratory frequency is being altered. You are functioning at a level that is different from that which you have functioned in the past. Indeed, many of you now are functioning at a level that you have never experienced in embodiment upon this planet before. And you say to me, "Thank you, that is well and good. I am quite happy to know this, but frankly this is not going to get me out of this muddle with my spouse. So what should I do?" Well, I cannot give you specific directions. May I offer some general guidelines for your consideration.

Each of you since you have begun your studies have heard the phrase, "of allowing ones to be". When you first heard these words, it seemed like what we heard was, "to be what? What does this mean, to be? There is something wrong with the communication pattern." And then as you have grown in your awareness you recognize to be is a totality. You are entering this vibratory change, this frequency change that you would allow others to be; to be able to accept them where they are and to recognize that they do not have the same needs, the same thought forms, the same desires as you. But that is there path.

This is also the period when many of you shall come out of the closet, so to speak. And you will stand on your beliefs. Now here may I say -- and I would underline this thought form for you -- <u>I am not saying that you would stand and you would spout to your spouse that the space brothers say this and such. Or that, "The Beloved Master taught us so and so."</u> There is a commonality of ground that you might use. And this commonality says to take the thoughts that are shared with you, the teachings that are shared with you and to share these thoughts. Love is a common thought. Love is a common thread -- caring about your brother; recognizing the gift of your environment that you would maintain its beauty and its virginity; being prepared for a seige of inclement weather or for Earth changes; universal truths; the Law of Cause and Effect. These are but examples of thoughts for conversations, for exchange of ideas that you might use with others in relationships.

You of your planet, particularly your western society -- I believe that is the term you us -- are great ones at a superficial talk. I believe you call it "small talk". Though I have yet to determine what has brought forth this particular size. If I were to give a size to it, I think I would call it great talk. For this is how you spend the majority of your energies as you would consciously converse with others upon your planet. It is as if each has built a wall around themselves. And they would choose not to let others know how they feel, what they experience, what realization has come to them. But they would choose to speak of the weather. And the females would choose to discuss the length of the skirt, of the garment. Or men would gather and they would speak of that which you call your sports, your games -- where one man or a team of men is pitted against another.

But those things which are very close to your hearts, those realizations that have come to you that you know are truth, these are not shared openly. But rather they are held as precious gems that are only shared with a very select group. And as your vibratory rate is altered you are finding that select group are ones that are also experiencing the vibratory change. But you can speak of many things in a general way, not to frighten, not to condemn, but to open a little door. Or shall I say open a door a little -- I believe that is the correct term. And as you would open that door a little so it is that light comes through the door. And as it would be opened wider, there is more light that comes, does it not? Do you get my point of that which I speak?

The basic thought is not new upon your planet. The communion that you each take for granted as we would speak with you is not a new communion. But it is one, shall we say that is a lost art by many ones upon the planet. And because it is lost, it is a frightening one. Yes, they shall become more tuned to it. But take the thoughts that have been shared. Take the love that is freely shared with you that each of you says you experience and you feel. Take this and share it with others in relationships.

But even as you would share these, know there are some that shall go the opposite direction from you because they are uncomfortable with your energy pattern. Bless these ones and let them be, just as you must be. And love all ones equally. For there are none greater and there are none less in the eyes of the Divine Creator. It is that you need a slight jiggling to help you become aware of relationships and what you are experiencing.

Some of you as your vibratory rate is altered may find that you are in a relationship that must come to a close. That may mean for you a tremendous lesson. For it may mean a time that you must be absolutely, totally, completely without blame; that you would not blame another in any way, but recognize that no longer can you walk side by side. And others of you shall be coming into new relationships, ones that shall be more close, more beautiful, more sharing and more expansive. For it is that you are coming into a communion with other ones that are walking at the same rate you are walking.

I merely bring these examples to you that you would be aware that as the energies are introduced to Mother Earth and to those of you that are with her, you are going to feel these. And as you feel these, others feel them. And each one acts and reacts in their own way. Do not condemn, but do not condone. Merely be all that you can be. And recognize that relationships do alter as your vibratory rate changes. For Earth is in a particular dimension, and at this time that dimension is expanding. Its parameters are expanding, and many of you are the ones that are pushing the parameters still farther out. Those that choose not to push the parameters out shall not be as comfortable in the thinner ethers.

I trust I have been able to as you would say, shed a small measure of light upon a subject that is dear to your heart. It is with great joy that I speak with you. And I trust the thoughts that I have shared have been ones that have been easy for you to comprehend. Recognize I am quite unfamiliar with putting thought forms into words. For indeed, your language is one that is quite new to me. I trust in the upcoming period that we might be able to speak again. And if I might be of assistance to you, please feel free to call upon me that I might assist...

I'd like to ask a question on sexual relationships. Over time there seems to be less of a desire for such relationships. Is that normal?

EMARTUS Let us look at that which is the sexuality known on planet Earth. It is a procreation situation, is it not? It is also an example in which the dualities or the extremes of the dualities come together -- the masculine and the feminine. They unite to bring forth another being. Can you also see this as representative of yourselves -- the masculine aspects and the feminine aspects coming forth to let you be a balanced being?

This particular method of procreation is used predominantly upon your planet. There are slight variations of it within your dimension, but in the other dimensions there is not the emphasis placed upon procreation in the way that it is placed upon your planet. There is a great indoctrination that goes on about your planet, with an emphasis on the differences of the two sexes rather than that which is coming together in the melding and growing within the oneness of the individual.

As your energy infusion began and you experienced this, many of you who are in masculine form, or in male form, have felt you have gone through a phase of feeling quite vulnerable, and indeed, you have found that you weep much more easily than you have done before. This is in direct relationship to the acceptance of the energies which have come to you because you are experiencing more of a balancing within your totality. The feminine aspects of your total being are coming forth more in a balancing manner. Hence, some of you are finding you are more nurturing than you were. You are seeing various characteristics within you coming up which would be interpreted as feminine characteristics. This causes a confusion in some in the mass consciousness upon your planet, because they do not understand what they are experiencing.

But what it is, is the sensitivity and attunement is coming forth in those who have been the doers and those who have chosen to close off this whole experience.

In contrast, those who are the feminine ones are finding a strength within them which they had not explored before. This was brought about several years ago upon your planet when you had this great wave of feminism, did you not, and the women worked very hard at being masculine? They dressed as their male counterparts; they entered into the competitive fields the same way as the males did; and indeed, you went through a period of great rivalry.

But see this as pendulums which are swinging with the introduction of energies that you experience the extreme before you come into a balance. And you are coming into a place of balance in which you can recognize the gifts and the attributes of each individual, regardless of whether they are masculine or feminine, male or female, recognizing that those masculine-feminine traits are coming into a balance within the individual. So as you do this, your sexual desires will decrease, because you are not seeking externally for gratification, but you are finding a balance within yourself and finding that that is where your strength is.

What about homosexuality?

JOKHYM ...You have a high consciousness in your day of that which is called homosexuality, do you not? How did this begin? It began with Atlantis. At the time of Atlantis, women were considered to be nil. Their primary responsibility was to bear children. The male was the dominant aspect of society. And the male in his "wisdom" -- and if you will note I will put that in little brackets -- decided that they did not need wo-man, that they could create a vehicle for children and they could bring about a superior race, a superior specie, if they could eliminate this weakness that was called wo-man.

So there was a great deal of experimentation done in laboratories etc., and man found that he was not physically set up, capable of carrying a young. At such time there was even an attempt to take the uterus or the womb from women and place it within man, and it was not successful. There was an attempt with animals, that perhaps the animal could carry the seed and they wouldn't need the wo-man. This is where you have gotten into this situation of man evolved from the apes. And so now at this point in your cycle you are find-ing again there are ones who have come into embodiment and though they are not carrying the same thought they car-ried at that time, there is still a predominance etc.

Cloning was done in your laboratories in Atlantis. Cloning has been done for a time, within your laboratories upon your country. This is not something that is new. This is being done. As I would term them, bio-robots are also in ac-tion upon your planet, though they are not acknowledged by the masses of your people. This was also done at the time of Atlantis. It is a repeat. Man is looking for an easy way out. Man is looking for power. The collective, the individuals are looking for power over others. And this is their way that they are coming about it, not recognizing man in himself has no power -- it is only the power he allows to flow through him from the Source of All that he grows in his own power, in his own strength.

Please comment on AIDS and homosexuality?

KEILTA Greetings in the Light of the Radiant One. ...I am hesitating because I would desire to put this in a framework, and the question that you ask could take many hours of your time for answer. But briefly I will share some thoughts with you. This condition that is known to you as AIDS is a result of the collective consciousness of Earth mankind of this hour. It was introduced by Earth man for Earth man.

That which is called your homosexuality is a state of awareness that has caused much confusion upon your planet. In most instances where there is a lasting relation-ship of ones of the same gender, there has been a past life association that has not been finished, that was ended abruptly and was not allowed to take its steps. You will note I preface this with those of a relationship that is a one-to-one relationship. In this instance, it is finishing out that which was started in another lifetime.

You will recognize that on your soul level there is no male or female. You are both, you are neither, however you would choose to say this. However you take on specific form when you come to your planet. In some instances, as the soul desired to come into the form they got confused on the form, which has caused confusion for them on your plane. But this speaks to that which is the lasting relationships.

There are those that would be called your social but-terflies, if that would be a correct term. These ones are responding to a lower chakra energy, and are not desiring to evolve along the heavenly, universal man evolvement, the hu-man evolvement, if you will. These ones are reacting, responding to the energies that are flowing through their form that are of a more, I believe your Earth term would be, base energies. Please do not condemn them, for that is where they are. This is their choice, and it is only as man holds out his hand for man to assist that all are elevated.

This which is the condition that is known to you as AIDS was introduced by mistake, shall we say, for indeed, it was originated in a test tube. Were you aware of that? That shall be another story another day. And it spread most quickly. As with all things, please look at them, not in a judgment of that which is good and that which is bad, but look at it in a total, non-judgmental way.

There are those that have come to your planet that have taken on this condition in order that they would absorb some of the collective karma of Earth man kind, or some of the karma of Mother Earth, that others would not have to go through this experience. And so, as you would look at one or another, you cannot give a pat answer that would cover all ones, for each is an individual situation.

Just as there are ones that have had that condition that is known to you as cancer, which has become a dreaded word upon your planet, there are ones that have terminated their life stream upon the planet by this particular condition in order that they would absorb some of the pain, so that Earth man kind, their brothers and sisters, would not have to. So, for some that would perhaps seem that they are walking a path that would not be compatible with yours, perhaps the path they are walking is one as a volunteer so that another's path would be smoother. Until the final count is in, so to speak, you cannot know.

If energy just is, then is it not up to us as to how we use it from a sexual energy point of view?

KEILTA This is very true, for energy Is, period. It is how you would choose to use the energy as to what effect it would have upon you. That which is known as your sexual energy's primary focus is that of re-creation, or procreation for the form that the soul will be housed in on the planet.

You are aware that on other planets there is procreation by other means than that which you enjoy upon your planet. And indeed, that experience that you have now is not the experience that you had at your beginnings when first this planet was here, before it had solid form. Indeed, as you would evolve -- and again I shall underscore this that, it is an individual growth, it is an individual process. As you would evolve you find that your energies would possibly, could possibly, in most cases are centered along a different avenue, and that which was considered solely a sexual relationship would not continue to have the meaning that it had had previously. In some instances, this allows for the opportunity of the growth of the relationship into one that covers more facets of the totality of the individuals. Here, as I said previously, this is an individual basis. This is on an individual level.

Those that are of other planets and galaxies are not as, shall we say, caught up in the sexuality of the relationship as you upon your planet are. We hold this in a different perspective, but we see the relationship between mates as the opportunity to assist each to grow in their own totality, that it would be a total experience, not a fragmented one. This is different than on your planet.

I will also add one thought that I had not added to your last comments. Though you upon your planet profess to believe in life eternal, you don't really believe it. You see yourselves as the termination as soon as the form quits responding. You do not see yourselves as eternal beings. Hence, there is a great fear of that which you call death. There have been ones that have been documented who have experienced the process of that which you would call death, and they have returned to your plane to tell you of glorious things, of wondrous experiences. And those that you have known that have had this experience, they are willing to leave of their form, but yet they have a great joy in that which they are. They know they are eternal. It seems that you that are in the form this hour do not truly believe that, but you see yourselves as the form, and when it leaves, you leave.

I bring this to your awareness, merely to illustrate the fact that be it any of the conditions that you have, these are but a wink of the eye in the eternity.

* * * * *

Once again, we have concluded our time with you. We desire that you have learned from this sharing. Be at peace until we come together again.

Sarna, out.

CHILDREN

Greetings dear ones. As you know, I am Sarna. This evening we would like to continue our discussion, but instead of having the adult as our focus, let us focus on the stage of development known to you as the child hu-man. Our speakers will be Ming-ling, Lady Nada and Lady Athena, Commanders Jokhym, Emartus, Monka, and me. Ming-Ling will be the first to speak.

* * * * *

Greetings in the Light of the Radiant One. I am Ming-Ling who would share with you...

The storm clouds of dissension seem to gather more and more momentum. Even though man speaks of peace and speaks of unification, many, many factions continue to be divided and torn. Governments are interrupting life streams merely because of that which they call religious differences or philosophies. Truly, in many of your places of your world man has not risen beyond the initial phase of his dimensional existence. It is our desire to see the Light of understanding, acceptance and love spread to cover the face of planet Earth. Yet we know this must be the desire of Earth mankind.

May I, at this moment, put forth the urgent plea to all ones: If you would not desire peace for yourself, do this for your children and your children's children. Allow them the opportunity to walk in Light. Allow them the opportunity to meet with the Golden Sun/Son. As you would war, one man against another, and indeed, brother with brother, bring to your consciousness the face of the small child and its silent plea for peace upon its land.

Children know no racial barriers. They have no ethnic preferences. Children see other children as brothers and companions. There is a simplicity in their approach. Cannot the big brothers and the big sisters who are to be their guides -- those who have prepared the way for the children -- can they not, but for a moment, gaze about themselves with the eyes of the small child?

We know, even as I share these thoughts with you, Earth man has chosen to experience the changing of the planet in his own way. But I put forth the plea to all ones who would receive of my thoughts to remember the children; to close their eyes and open them so they may gaze about themselves with the wonder and the joy and the expectation with no judgment, with no division, even as the small child does this. This would assist Earth man as he comes into grips with the vibrations and the vibrational patterns introduced to him. Be as the child.

Beloved brothers and sisters of Earth, I speak to you now as a representative of your brothers and sisters of Venus. We are a sister planet to you of Earth. No, we do not experience the upheavals which are enjoyed upon your planet, for indeed, we are a more peaceful, pastoral civilization. We are ones who honor life the wonderful, wondrous gift in all things. We, too, share of our energies, our being, to assist you upon your planet in your stabilization, in your process, your wondrous process. May you soon come into that which is your birth by divine right.

I am your sister, a most humble servant of the I AM. I am Ming-Ling.

* * * * *

Greetings, beloveds of Earth. I am known as Nada. Yes, I have been chohan of the rays. And now, I have entered into that service which is to work with ones of the dimensions that are known to you as your brothers and sisters of space, that I might serve more closely, that I might serve with you.

I have walked of your plane. I have loved as you

have loved, for I have had husband and I have had children. And I have had mother and I have had father. I know of that which you feel for I have experienced the same. And even as I have had of these ones and I have held them within my heart in love so has there been a greater love within me and so has that love grown. For this is the love of my Creator, of our Father, our Mother, our God.

I would choose to speak with you of love. I would call this the parents love. And there are those of you that would say to me, "I am no longer a parent for my little birds have flown the nest." And there are others that would say to me that, "I have not experienced this love, this parents love, for I have not been a parent." I would speak of the parent that is the parent of your creation, the Father-Mother, and you, which are, each of you, a Son of God. You, the three of you establish a triune, for you are a Divine Child. And this parent, this Godhead sent forth this small Perfect Essence, a drop of pure Golden Love, and blest this drop and said, "Manifest of your creation." That is what you are, this pure golden drop of Love.

And now, as portion of the triune with the Divine Father-Mother, you are asked to represent the perfection of your parents. And this love that you are, that they have sent forth, knows no limits, knows no boundaries, sees no error, hands down no judgments. It merely is there for you, for you to take from this to be nourished, to grow. And as you would grow, you experience. And at times you are as the small child and you crawl a distance from your parents, and your parent waits for you mostly lovingly and most patient, until as the small child you cry. And your parent comes and lifts you.

And then as you grow, you no longer crawl away, but you walk or you run in halting steps. Again as your cry goes forth as you fall, your parent lifts you up most lovingly, caresses you, and heals your scars, your wounds. This parent has set you free, but yet this parent is always with you. This parent allows you to be. There is no judgment. There is no price asked but to love. And this one is always there regardless of how many times you would turn your face away. This one is with you.

And as you grow, and you feel you have outgrown the lap of your mother or the knee of your father, you would weep in your pillow oft times at your loneness. And still they come to comfort you. And yea, they send others to walk with you or to sing you the lullaby that you would hear the song.

This one, this Divine Parent, have created for you all that you need, all that you desire. And they have given you the ability to create also. For you as you know your needs, as you know your desires can create that which would quench your desires. For this Divine Parent would desire that you want for nothing. They would want that you would manifest what they have given to you at your beginning, where you are at this moment. You may take side trips, and you may desire to create that which once you have created it, you don't want it any more. But they are there. They offer no judgment. They offer acceptance. They ask of you nothing except to be that which you were at your creation.

You may put on many layers, many, many layers over this Divine Portion, and they see through this. They see what you truly are, and they watch you grow. And they watch as you manifest that which is your beginning. And they too grow as you grow for they are the seed that is within your heart, for they have planted that seed there. And as you would lay upon your cot, and you would slumber so does your Mother come and sing to you the sweetest lullaby. And so does your Father whisper to you and say, "Well done My Son, well done. Manifest of Me that all of our creation would feel of our nearness. Manifest of Me." And you, beloved golden essences, open your eyes from your slumber, and the still small voice within your heart says, "Beloved Father, beloved Mother, may I this day walk with my hand in Yours that I truly would manifest that which You are and that which You have given me to be."

For you see, dear ones, it was given for you to be

perfect, even as your Parents are perfect. Recognize, remember, always remember, you are a triune of the Divine Triune for you are the Son of the Father-Mother God. Hold this to your hearts, my beloved ones, hold this to your hearts.

Can you tell us what a mother-to-be can do to assist the child she is carrying?

EMARTUS Greetings and salutations. ...Recognize that there has been a bond between the parents, the soul of the parents, and the soul of that one which would take embodiment. The primary responsibility for this one that is the mother that would carry a child within their womb is to maintain a housing that is as pure as can be in every aspect. May this mother be one of peace. May she fuel her form with that which are the natural foods, those which are the living foods. And may she speak with this one that she carries and tell them of where they are coming and share of the love that she has for that one.

As she would also maintain her own peace by reading, by growth, by that which you call meditation or quietness, rest, and generally maintain a well-being, a balance within her totality, hence, that which is the soul of the one that is coming in feels of this welcome that has been prepared, and there is a bonding that has already been experienced before the soul has entered totally into the form.

Do the babies have a highly developed soul when they come in, and does their spirit travel back and forth in sleep state as we are told that we as adults do?

JOKHYM Salutations, my brothers and sisters of planet Earth. ...Indeed, your spirit, your spirit vehicle, does go forth as your being sleeps or is quiet for long periods in contemplation. Many of you have traveled aboard our ships in such state, and you have recollection of that which you have seen.

This you know and you are aware of.

But now let us take one that you call an infant upon your plane. The divine essence enters of this being at the time of birth, of the birthing process. Yes, the divine essence and its experiences, that which is known to you as the soul is close by during the total period that the infant is in utero, for it observes the parents, it observes the surroundings, and in most instances accustomizes itself to that which it is coming to. You will note those that have made a satisfactory adjustment are those infants that seem quite happy with themselves. And you will also recognize there are ones that seem quite unhappy with their surroundings and where they are. Perhaps these were not as eager to enter this embodiment, and they have come in, so to speak, and they are setting up a ruckus.

Your soul, as it is within a small infant child on your planet, is allowed a good measure of freedom, for its experiences initially in the first few weeks of its habitation upon your planet are quite limited. Therefore, the soul gathers its experiences outside of the physical vehicle. Then as the infant grows and becomes more aware consciously of its surroundings and those that are with it and its sensory mechanisms bring in the varying stimuli, so it is that the soul begins to adjust, to live within that physical vehicle. You must recognize, that this is not an easy transition for one that has been allowed to travel as the wind to all of a sudden abruptly to be housed in this small cramped little vehicle that goes nowhere. So thus the soul is allowed a measure of experiences so that this transition process is a gradual one and is not one that is too traumatic.

The soul is not an infant. The soul that enters through the infant vehicle is one that has lived many life times, and has a great storehouse of knowledge with it. It is frustrating for this one to be in this vehicle that cannot communicate with others upon its plane. For you see, the soul has enjoyed a wide and varied thought communication. But as it has entered of this vehicle, these ones that are with it, that nourish it, that clean it, that love it, do not communicate in the same way that the soul is familiar with. So there is a certain amount of frustration. This too is evidenced by the loud wailing that an infant produces.

As there is a soul contact established with the parenting vehicles, there is a greater soul communication. Thus there is not as not as great a need for the soul to go out for its communication. Thus, as the stimuli come into the sensory motors of the vehicle, then there is an establishment of the link between the parenting souls and the new one that has just come forth. This assists this one to live, so to speak, in this new vehicle...

How can a mother help a child to expand the visions, the feelings that they have, rather than suppress it to make them fit into the reality as we say it is, and for the child to be comfortable to come to the mother and talk about these things?

NADA ...That which is called your child, recognize is a small form for a great being. For you must recognize that your soul and that which is the soul of your children have set up the experience of your coming together, and you have elected to be a tool in order to bring them into this dimension that you are in. Until a child has reached approximately eighteen months of age upon your planet their soul goes back and forth freely. It is not bound with the form, but there is the adjustment period as it may go back and forth. You will note, many of you have good babies that have slept long periods of time. It is because the divine portion is in school on another plane or dimension.

But it is at approximately that which would be considered one-and-a-half of your calendar years that the soul says, "Very well. I will stay with this form." And so it is that it begins to experience the limitation of the physical form. You will also note at that time the child becomes more inquisitive about what is going on on your plane. It is understood the mothers say, "They begin to get into everything", is it not? And so it is though the child still has, the divine portion still has the ability to go forth, at certain periods within their life, within your life, there is still the travel back and forth. But there is not as much of it done, until gradually it would be about that which you would call your age of puberty that the soul is locked into the earth experiences.

When the young one, the child, begins to speak to their parents of things that they see, of things that they know, or that which they understand -- and oft times the parents will say the child has a very good imagination, they have an active imagination -- the child gradually learns that this is not necessarily a good thought, so they shut down, so to speak. But as a parent, as a child will share these thoughts with you, accept them. Talk to them of these experiences. Talk to your children of the angels. Talk to them of the elementals. Many children are very comfortable with the elemental kingdom, for indeed, they see these ones. There are those which are books that are coming forth that have been guided to be put into print that speak of the elemental kingdom, that speak of the angelic kingdom in such ways that children are comfortable with them. Read these stories to them.

Always impress upon your child their own value, their own worth, and that their thoughts are honored. There is no put-down for that which the child would say. And most of all, hold your children close to your heart. Let them know they are truly loved, they are welcomed to the plane, and they are appreciated for that which they contribute.

It is recognized that you must put specific parameters upon your children because of the society that you are in. Do this in a loving manner, with as few restrictions as you can. And again, enforce these with love that the child may understand the limits are for their own safety, their own growth, and that regardless of what they say or they do, that those which are their parents love them and honor them for what they are and what they contribute.

So how can we help re-initiate their visions, their feelings once it seems to be shutting down?

NADA Again, teach your children that home is a haven. It is a safe place to be who they are. Home is a sacred place. Teach them to respect themselves and teach them to respect others. And know that that which is shared within the walls of their home is shared as a trust with those that share of their home, and that this trust will not be violated.

You can begin with these children by reading stories, and though sometimes they would say they are too big for a story, you may perhaps open the door to a discussion. "Have you thought about....". And a small boy will say to you at the age of six, there are no such things as fairies. You as a parent, can you say to them, "I believe in them. I believe in fairies, and there are people that can see them." It does not have to be said in a dogmatic manner, but it is what you would call "planting seeds". You merely would plant the seed and see what sort of soil that it would fall upon. And perhaps you would find that another day that this one might pick up a book and bring to you and say, "Is this one about fairies?" It does not have to be done in a threatening manner. It is merely that you would plant a seed, that the door would not have to be closed for them.

ATHENA Greetings in the Light of the Source to each of you. It is my joy that I would come and I would speak. You would speak of the children and indeed this is a subject that is close to my heart.

These ones, as has been written in many books, are special ones since that which is your year 1965. These ones come with great gifts and attributes. As a parent your responsibility for these ones is to help them grow. They are ones that need guidance, they need to be steered, if you will, along certain ways. They would react very strongly to that which is the strong hand of discipline that has been used most handily upon your planet. Their biological needs, you will note are different than those which would be their older brothers and sisters for indeed they react to many of the foodstuffs that you have taken for granted. They have minds that are very inquisitive and they would not desire to be locked into the traditional systems that you have grown accustomed to on your planet. They have inquisitive minds, they learn quickly for they are used to being in a school where they are challenged and they are allowed to express in their own growth process.

These ones, as I have said, react to many of the foods upon your planet. You will find that they are more closely tuned to their own biological needs than perhaps you who are their parents. And you will find one that will eat a great quantity of one food, and then perhaps a great quantity of another food because it is they are working in their own balancing system...

ATHENA (continues) ...The small ones that have come since that which would be your year 1980 are ones that have come quite unique. There are angelic ones that have taken on being in order to come and to bring a love, anchor the love upon your planet. These ones have a very close attunement to their Creation, to where they were before they have entered this embodiment. They have a great awareness. We would strongly urge the parents of these ones to let them stay as aware and open as possible. They might speak of the ships and they might speak of the dance of the angels that they observe. For they can share with you an understanding that will be a confirmation for many things that you would read in books but you have forgotten that you have experienced.

These ones need great fluids, a high fluid intake. The small ones need foods that are easily digestible. They need a minimum of stimulants, that which would be your caffeines, your sugars. And this is not to say that they can have none of these but rather that their diets be monitored so that there are ample natural foods within them.

Could you discuss the irritability of some of the children?

ATHENA This, shall we say, irritability in behavior patterns are a result of the sensitivity to the electromagnetic pull and what is going on on your planet at this time. And as you will note, the small ones will have periods of irritability. And if you will check, there have been geophysical changes going on about your planet, for they have a sensitivity to this. These are very sensitive ones that have come, they are very closely tuned. They have a very sensitive vibratory pattern that is easily influenced by what is going on about them.

How can we help them deal with this?

ATHENA Love these ones. Nurture them, love them, and see the Light that they are, guiding them as they need your guidance and sharing with them the wisdom that you have acquired concerning your planet. For indeed, they come as ones not quite sure of where they've come and what they should do and they are impatient ones. So, they need your guidance and the temperance that you would share with them.

Could you share some information on devic children?

SARNA There are ones that have taken embodiment on planet Earth and they are ones that have come into another state of evolution, because they have reached, or almost reached, the potential within their own kingdom. Some of these have produced great challenges for those that are their parents, for indeed they are living in two worlds simultaneously. These ones have chosen to come in to experience what man is experiencing in order that they might have the opportunity to go from the devic kingdom into a higher evolution of the angelic form by having the opportunity to come into that which is known to you as the physical form. The number of embodiments that they shall experience are not a great number of embodiments, for this is an embodiment opportunity to allow them to evolve more quickly within their own specific pattern.

These ones as they are within embodiment upon your planet have their feet in two worlds. It is a confusing situation for some of them initially. And as they grow to adulthood, some of them can be rather questioning, argumentative. In your earthean terms, they could be judged rather obnoxious for they do want to know. They do want to understand.

Then there are those that are on the other end of the continuum that are, as you would say, the little angels, for truly this is the reflection that is seen from their countenance. These ones have come to learn, they have come to share. They have great gifts and great understanding. And most of them are in a process of trying to assimilate the embodiment that they are in, plus the understanding and the wisdom that they have brought with them. They require a great nurturing, a great understanding.

And for those that are their parents, in most instances, they require a great deal of patience. You the parents, and the children, can learn from one another, and it can be a great time of growth and sharing.

What could we say to the children when they report seeing entities wearing black who scare them? And who are these entities?

SARNA As the question is shared, I feel the love that is poured forth in a concern, in a desire to protect those that are known to you as the children.

131

These ones that would come to the children are manifested thought forms. And indeed, at times, might be specific entities that are trying to create a state of unbalance and confusion within the small ones that they might be more vulnerable or have easier access by ones of the Dark Robes.

May we encourage each of you, and may you encourage each of your small ones to stay enfolded in the Light. Call forth the shield of protection. Place your mantle firmly about your shoulders and stay within your field of Light. Indeed, if you feel you are in a situation of uncertainty, see your field of Light and protection expand out through you that you are completely enfolded in it.

As the energies are coming to Earth, many entities are taking this opportunity to communicate with you upon your planet. Always, I repeat, always ask of one, "Do they come in Light?" There is a Cosmic Law that demands, that indeed dictates, if that is the word you would use, they must answer in truth.

Even though this must be answered in truth there are ones of the Dark Robes that have an evasive way of doing this. Always enclose anyone that comes to you in the Light of the Divine One. Just as you would enfold yourself in this Light, enfold all ones that would come to you in this same Light. The ones of the Dark Robes do not tolerate this and they will leave you.

It is with the small ones as they cry, or they react in a fearful way that they let their shields of protection down that the ones of the Dark Robes might tantalize them. Remind the small ones, even as you would remind yourselves, to keep your shields and your protection on. For this indeed is a trying period as the ones of the Dark Robes would seek to add to their numbers through those that are already in physical form upon your planet. For it is only as they have opportunity to work through those of the physical form that they might recruit the highest numbers. And they are on a great recruitment at this time.

I'm concerned about some of the rock groups and their impact on the young ones. Would you speak of this?

MONKA I greet you in the Light of the Source. ...There are many ways that are used by the Dark Brotherhood to sway, to impress, to use man of Earth. One way that this is done is by some of the current trends in your so-called music. Other ways that this is done is by the subliminal messages on your media called television. Still other ways that this is done is by the omission and the warping of facts as they are presented in your newspapers. The ones of the Dark Brotherhood use every available resource to ensnare, to add to their numbers.

The battle upon your earthly plane at this time is a most heated one, and we recognize the precarious position of you of Earth that are called parents. We recognize that the burden you carry is not an easy one for you know of the Light, and you know of the path that should be followed. And yet you have within your protection and your supervision many that you would call rebels. Am I not correct? Yes, I know I am. And though you would seek to guide and you would seek to impress these ones you feel that you are speaking to a closed door, for outwardly you receive no confirmation in your mutual exchange of thoughts. In fact you feel no mutual exchange.

Might I say to you as you live the example that you would have your young ones follow, as you speak to them of truth and in truth, and as you manifest love to them and for them, this is the greatest lesson they can follow. This is the greatest lesson they receive. And yes, there are ones that shall be swayed by many of these so-called music groups who are manifestations of the Dark Brotherhood. And these have chosen of this path. For you must remember these ones that are placed within your responsibility -- that you see as babies, as small souls that you hold in your arms -- in truth these are individual souls that have been placed within your trust for a period of time. But each must walk of its own path.

Because of the closeness of the end of your cycle,

133

and because all things on Earth have been speeded up by Earth man, these ones that you call children are in actual fact growing older much more quickly than you realize. And as you would speak with them, you shall find that there is a wisdom within them that is beyond their years. Yes, there are ones that are caught up by the ones of the Dark Brotherhood, but the number is far less than those who see of what is transpiring for what it actually is, and that feel of what truth is, that feel of love, and that walk with this.

You must forgive my expounding on this subject, but as one who is and was a parent, I feel most closely to each of you that are struggling in bringing forth these souls to their appointed age on Earth. The joy is great. The pain is greater. And none can know what the path is of this soul that has entered embodiment until that time that that soul comes before the board and says, "This I did, and this I omitted."...

In some of the material that I have read, there has been mention of satanism, and the use of children and animals as sacrifices. It seems that our children are susceptible to the teachings and the influences about. Could one of you comment on this, please?

MONKA I too weep at Earth man's abuse of these ones that have been placed within his charge. There are ones upon your planet that are consumed by the dark ones. There are ones upon your planet at this hour, that are the dark forces manifested in form. These ones have no conscience as you would speak of, as you would use this term. These ones are consumed with the carnal pleasures, and with the elevation of the ego. They are bound, are tied, are weighted totally to the earthly plane and to the lower dimensions, to that which is the lowest of the physical being.

I would add here, a note of light for each of you that you might draw comfort within your heart. For know that each child that is not enfolded in parental love is enfolded in our love and our protection. And though the physical being may be in the most extenuating circumstances, the soul is lifted above this that there is no scarring, that there is no pain. For these ones have come forth in a state of innocence, and they have come forth in a state of pleasant expectation. And these ones are cared for both by the angelic realms, and by those ones that we send forth also.

Yes, there is sadness in our hearts, but know also my brother, that as you express concern so is your concern and your caring taken upon wings, that it goes forth to minister, to soothe, to comfort those that would cry in sleepless nights.

* * * * *

Our discussion with questions and answers has concluded for this particular portion. We trust you are beginning to see the interrelationship of one with another upon your planet, recognizing one does not act independently but rather as part of a large consciousness. Does this not help to expand the concept of Brotherhood? I will leave you with that thought.

Sarna, out.

THE ANIMAL KINGDOM

      I greet you and welcome you in the Light of our Radiant one. When we have gathered earlier we have spoken about the hu-man, its child and the relationship with the Earth Mother. The question has been put forth concerning the animals, those who live in independence and those who have established a close relationship with you. What of these ones? Tonight, we will address that concern. Our speakers will be Soltec, Aleva, and Keilta. I will be your coordinator. You may begin your questions.

Could you talk to us about the animals on the planet and what we can do to help them?

SOLTEC Greetings, my brothers and sisters of planet Earth. ...My first comment to you would be to recognize that there is no emphasis that is placed on one above the other, but there is a great interrelationship that is going on. The extinction of many of the animal life forms upon your planet are not solely -- and that is not intended as a pun, I assure you -- the result of the misuse of man kind. But rather, specific species have been removed for their own protection that they might again return to Earth when there is a more harmonious state.

      There are animals that have been -- and animals, this is a word that is quite interesting, for indeed, are you not considered an animal also? -- but there are ones, shall we say, that have been entrusted to you, that are the God representatives upon your planet, that have been misused and have been abused. These ones have left, or are leaving, and they are enjoying a habitation in another galaxy.

      The soul essence of those which are your flesh-eating

animals has -- I cannot use the term "reincarnated", because this is not the path that the animal would take -- but the soul essence has taken in the form, has gone into the form in another galaxy of an animal that is not flesh-eating, for animal or man was not intended to eat flesh. This was done as an interim period. For these that have been relocated, there has been an educational process that has been going on for them that they might be ready to again return to the planet after it has gone through its geophysical changes.

Man, in his evolutionary process upon your planet, has come into the recognition of his superiority, but he has not accepted the responsibility and the trust that was placed within him. Hence, there has been that which you would call animals that have been abused, have been misused. There are many more that have been removed from your planet than you realize -- many species, such as those which would fly in your skies, or dwell upon the face of Mother Earth. For they have been afforded the comfort of being uninvolved as much with man and his evolution. However, as the larger mammals were discovered by man and their form was used for oil, for foodstuffs, etc., they, too, have felt the impact of man's selfishness.

That which is called your pollution is now having -- and this is not something that has happened within just the past few of your calendar years, but this has been a most grave process for the last quarter of your century, in that the waters have been polluted. That which would be called your fishes have adapted, have died. And these species have become unknown because man never had the opportunity to enjoy them. He has destroyed them. This is observed by us.

Those that are of the animal kingdom that have the greatest potential, and by this, the determination is that which was their intent, the thought by which they came forth, these have been removed and they are in safe-keeping until such time as man can live in harmony with them.

We, within the Fleet, monitor this which is your animal

137

kingdom, just as Mother Earth, herself, is monitored, as is your plant systems, to determine the level of support that there is for an harmonious interrelationship upon the planet.

That which are known as animals are placed on planet Earth to be comfort, to be companion to that which is known as man that walks the planet. It is only as man has digressed from his own original purpose that he, too, has allowed his relationship with the animal to digress.

Those which would be of an evolution that would not allow them to return to a form that would be compatible with Cosmic Law are, indeed, being absorbed into the oversoul until such time as a new formation would come forth that would be of a gentler nature. This has been the result because of man's attitude with the animal. But rest assured, there are many ones that have been removed for their own safekeeping and for the preservation until such time as you upon the planet are ready to live with them in peace.

Each of you, regardless of where you live or what you are doing, can hold your animal kingdom in love. You can project the thought that will protect them, that they will be watched over, that no harm will come to them. You can do this for that which would be called your seal or your polar bear, though you may never actually see the animal itself. You may visualize the animal, see it in its own level of Light, and see it smile, and know that it is protected and loved. And you have the ability to do this, regardless of where you live or what your lifestyle is. You do not have to specifically touch the animal in order to express your love and your concern for them, but you can do this by projecting of your thought.

What of the soul of animals as compared to the soul of man?

SARNA If you would, in your mind's eye, picture the great, omnipotent Light -- for indeed, that which is Creator Source is beyond that which can be described for your comprehension -- and of that great, magnificent Light, there is a portion of that Light that goes forth. It would be as a small spark, and that small spark has entered a form within a specific dimension. Now that spark will stay in that form as long as the form is of use. But then when the form begins to wear and is of no longer a vehicle of growth for the little spark, then the vehicle is laid down -- that which you would call die, death. And the spark then goes forth to another dimension. This is what you are, you are the divine spark. You have come directly from the Creator. You are the closest thing to Creator that can be experienced by anything else within your dimension. Now hold that thought and see yourself as that little spark.

That which would be your pets, those which are the other animal kingdoms upon your planet, these ones do not come forth with an individual spark, but rather, they are a projection. And they would have what would be called by you as an oversoul, or there is one soul for all of those that you would call your canine or your dog kingdom. And when their form is laid aside, then they would return to that which is the oversoul or the larger soul that is of their species.

Now, if there would be that which would be one that is a portion of that oversoul that has a very strong bond with you that are the divine spark, this one might reincarnate again as that which would be your dog, to be with you, to serve with you, to assist you, perhaps to take care of you. In many instances of that which are known as your seeing eye dogs, these ones have incarnated specifically to take care of the one without vision, for perhaps in another lifetime that one has taken care of them when they were not able to take care of themselves in one way. Perhaps it might be that the canine could not hear or could not see. And so they would come out of love that they would perform the same for another. Do you understand the difference?

All is Creator. ...That which are your pets -- and we have spoken of that which is the dog, we will continue with that example -- they do not enjoy the ability to attain the Christed position, but rather, theirs is a portion of evolution. And the oversoul that is the canine oversoul does not evolve into the Christed state, but rather, this one would assist others, such as yourself, to attain that position.

...I would urge each of you to remember, that there is no less, there is no greater, there is no higher, there is no lower. There is but that which is Creator. And each has a purpose and each assists the other...

There seem to be a lot of animals dying, such as the great numbers of birds and fish in Nevada. Could you comment?

ALEVA Hello, hello, hello. I would greet each of you most humbly in the Light of the Radiant One.

...Well, is it any wonder? Just look what you do there. Just look at what you have released within the Earth as you would test all your explosions and all of your nuclear devices. You have upset the balance of your planet, and it is quite intense in this area. And these ones cannot tolerate such an imbalance. It is part of the change that is coming about. But it is also greatly induced by the carelessness of ones of your government as they would choose to test their nuclear devices and their warheads within the ethers and under the ground within the planet. This must stop. For the good of all ones upon your planet, for all life forms upon your planet, it must stop.

You have no idea how many times we have interceded that there would not be a detonation or an explosion. Or missiles have been stopped in mid-air. Or silos -- that's a word that tickles me -- your silos would not open up to allow your missiles to come forth. For we have closed them. We have done this in an effort to assist you upon your planet, to assist all life forms upon your planet.

Would you comment on why some species of whales are beaching themselves, and why Man has the relationship

he has with dolphins?

KEILTA Greetings, dear ones of planet Earth. ...There is a two-fold reason of the activity that is going on within these ones that are inhabitants of your oceans. One is the feeling, the knowing, the understanding of these ones who have a high intelligence level of the cyclic conclusion at this time. And so they would desire to come forth to communicate with you, Earth Man, for indeed, there has been a communication link between you o'er eons of habitation. These ones have merely chosen to inhabit in these particular forms.

The other reason that there are ones that are choosing to terminate their physical embodiment upon the planet is that they have concluded the experiences that they have needed in order to reach a higher state of evolution. And therefore, because they are at the end of the cycle they have the opportunity to leave of the form in a more expedient manner than going through a total embodiment process. And so it is, as the divine portion would leave of the form, they have come to shore.

That which is known as your dolphin is a most intelligent co-habitant with you. And indeed, there is much that this one, this particular species, might share with you. When you have reached a state that you are able to understand and to enter into an appreciative state of communication with these ones, you will find that there are specific keys that have been given to these ones that are most valuable in treating specific conditions, particularly those which are known as your emotional unbalances. For these ones do not recognize that there is the unbalance, but rather, there is an energy force that goes through them to establish a balanced state within another.

They are eager to share their understanding with you. For indeed, their evolution has been one that has gone beside yours and they are most desirous to share these experiences that they too might evolve further along their cycle as that which they would share would assist you as you would go along your evolutionary cycle. Thus, the coming together and the mutual sharing would be beneficial to both.

SOLTEC That which is known to you as the whale and the dolphin, these are unique brothers and sisters of Earth Mankind. Even as they have come upon the shores, they have said to you the environment you are in and the one they are in is not compatible for habitation. They are saying to you they are leaving your planet because they can no longer function and because their function is no longer necessary. They too will return even as you return in a distant day. But they have earned a rest. They have earned this, and indeed this is what is happening.

There are those of you who would have a great sadness at the oil spill off your Alaskan coast and off your other coastal waters, and you would cry, weep tears at the number of animals and fishes who have given up their life. Are you aware there are animals and fishes which swam miles and miles and miles in order to enter into that oil slick? Now, why would they do that? Because this was their opportunity to leave your planet that they might have a rest, that they might be able to go forth to be armed in a new vibration and be ready to return to your planet.

So it is there is joy in all that happens. Even as those which are known to you as your brother and sister dolphins leaped into the nets, so it was their time upon your planet had been completed and they had no need of the form to take with them and they asked for the release. This was the method that was used. These ones will be working with you when you have returned. Indeed there are those who are waiting to enter the waters and the streams.

The elemental population is decreasing because of the lack of acknowledgment, the abuse of that which they hold in consciousness and the general neglect that is going on by you who they see as representatives of the divinity of that which is the Source of Being.

142

You have a celebration (Earth Days) upon your planet in which ones have come together and they have decried that which has been done to the Earth Mother and that which is being done. You have spoken of recycling and various other ways to help. I cannot over-emphasize the importance of this level of consciousness, for it is most important for all of you, not one day, but <u>every day</u>. If you would walk down your street and you would see that which has been placed there by another in carelessness, pick it up. Let the Earth Mother know by such an act of your respect and love for her. It is a simple thing.

This consciousness which has been brought to the forefront most recently is indeed a positive aspect for the planet. However, simply recycling your cans is not the answer for cleaning up your planet, healing its scars, neutralizing your wastes, it is but the beginning of an awakening. Each of you can do much in your consciousness by helping to clean up and to work with and to heal these places, these gouges, these scars that are within the surface of the Earth Mother.

* * * * *

Ladies and gentlemen, this concludes this portion of our discussion. I trust each has learned a small portion. When we next come together we will speak of the potential which lies within you and methods of attaining it. Go in peace and love.

Sarna, out.

REACHING OUR FULL POTENTIAL

Good evening, my compatriots. So it is that we once again come together. It would seem that our numbers are growing. Perhaps we shall have to enlarge the town hall's meeting room. This evening Lord Dionus, Commanders Ashtar, Monka, Jokhym, Hatonn and Captain Keilta and I will lead the discussion on reaching your potential.

* * * * *

Greetings dear ones, Ashtar here. It is with joy that I have the opportunity that I might blend energies with you...

To recognize your full potential is to realize your Christ state, or to realize the Christ dimension. To recognize that which you are capable of doing at this time requires periods of quiet, of deep searching within, of pondering, of a oneness of commitment to achieve your Christ self, to be in tune with all that is the creative process, all that is about you, and to be in absolute balance and harmony. This is not a state that you shall easily achieve, for this is one that you shall strive for. And those of you that would make a conscious, concerted effort shall find that you effort has been well worth it.

There are many of us that continue to strive for such a state of bliss, of at-one-ment. Recognize that we have evolved beyond that state in which you are in. But we too have not realized our full potential, for this is an ever ongoing upward spiral to the perfect dimension, to that which you know as the Total, or the Total Creative Force. Those that are known to you as the Hierarchy, those that are known to you as the Masters, those that are known to you as Ascended Beings, as Saints and Angels, have achieved a much higher level of attunment than we have, or many of us have.

However, there are ones that serve with us that have achieved a specific state that is far above those of others. Each travels of their own particular path, their own particular evolution as it has a balance and a comfort for them. Each of us in your dimension, as well as ours, strives for the absolute at-one-ment with the Creative Principle. This is our goal. This is the realization of what we really are. And may we, at some point within the cycle achieve this goal. And we would wish of this for each of you... I would say to you the quietness, the self search that is within you will reveal much of that which is beyond you.

My brothers and sisters of planet Earth, it is with joy that I have spoken with you of this hour...

Will we then be able to do teleportation and levitation?

MONKA Greetings, beloveds. ...There are many ones at this time upon the planet that have great and wonderful desires such as teleportation, levitation, materialization. There are others that would desire to know great mysteries and great secrets. And regardless of which school that you are following, you would desire instant success in your endeavors. You would desire to go from point A to point B with no regard of what is in the space between and the steps that must be taken. You would desire to have all knowing placed at your finger tips. And indeed, as we talk about changes and coming events, you would desire to have date, time, and place, and preferably those that were involved and what they were wearing at the time.

Dear man of Earth, it cannot work that way. For so much depends upon you and what you do and how you do it. Yes, there are specific changes that take place, that are taking place, that have taken place, and that will take place upon your planet. But it is up to you when these things shall happen. Yes, there is a sequence of events that shall be followed, just as there is a sequential pattern to your evolution, and no steps will be omitted.

Before you can get into teleportation or levitation or materialization there has to be some work done with you. First, is your desire, your motive a pure one? Or is it for novelty that you would like to do this? Do you recognize the responsibility, that it is part of your evolution? And that, in order to bring about these changes you must, your physical vehicle, go through specific molecular alteration.

And you say to me, "Ah, that's scary. What have you got in mind?" It is quite simple. Your vibratory rate must be altered as you grow in your own awareness, as you grow in your own Light centeredness. Each of you is going through a change. Each of you is becoming Lighter. You are less dense than you were. But you are not as Light as you can be or you shall be.

You have heard great and wonderful stories of ones that are standing before you and then "poof" all of a sudden they are not there. And they are somewhere half way across your planet. Well and good. But there is a responsibility to being able to do this. There is a purity of heart, of motive that is necessary.

And there are ones that would say, "If I could manifest, I would be a great healer." Would you heal another and deny them their rights? Would you step in to heal one and take on their karma? You can do this if you attempt to heal another without full knowledge of what you are doing. And you say to me, "If I could bring about a materialization, I would feed the world, and there would be none that would hunger." Do you recognize you have the food stuffs now that you can feed the world and there are none that hunger? So how can it be that you would need to do this? You already have that which you need.

You must first come into a state of peace. You must first come into a state of at-one-ment with the Creator Source, and maintain that state. Against all odds, maintain that state. And then, enter in to this molecular rearrangement, for that is what teleportation, levitation, precipitation, that is what these are, molecular rearrangement! Enter into these cautiously, always attuned to the Divine Will.

Most of you are quite eager to be able to do these feats because they are a "to do". And look at all the money you would save on tickets if you could teleport from one place to another.

First you must be aligned with the Divine Will, constantly aligned with Divine Will. Be filled with the Eternal peace and hold no thoughts that are not of balance and at-one-ment. Learn that lesson and then speak to me of your desire for the next portion. The horse cannot pull the cart if you have placed the cart before the horse. And this is what you are doing, my compatriots. In your eagerness, in your enthusiasm, you are attempting to skip a few steps. Each step must be learned carefully.

And there shall be ones that shall criticize you. And there shall be others that shall be most eager to offer their advice, their thoughts on what you should and you should not do. But it is up to each one to come into the realization of what their own path is and their own alignment with Creator Source. Disregard these ones, bless them, and be true to that which you are.

Light workers upon planet Earth are entering a state of seige, for you are coming out of your closets. You are standing firmly and saying what you believe and why you believe it. And this is most unsettling to many ones, and they would taunt you. And they would say, "If you have all these wonderful powers, well, do this and do that. Make this appear and that appear. Make this disappear and that disappear." Do not get caught in this game, my dear ones, for those that are sure within themselves do not have to prove themselves to anyone. As long as you are aligned with the Divine Will, and you know of your at-one-ment you do not have to prove this to others. They will sense it and they will know.

But what about all the information about us ascending?

DIONUS Greetings, my beloved ones of Earth. ...As you review, you will note ones have given specific dates concerning energy infusion in which you will automatically rise into the next dimension, you will have immediate alteration of vibrational pattern, and in some instances there is even offered immediate ascension. In each instance, the alteration in vibrational pattern is shown as one which will do a thing to you, not to allow you to do your own growth. This is an erroneous thought.

You are in a plane of free choice, one in which you have the opportunity to demonstrate Divine Will. To do anything to you is to transgress of the Law of Cause and Effect. No thing can be done to you without your own consent and preparation. Recognize as vibrational patterns are altered, you have opportunity to grow or to experience alteration. You, because you are in a plane of polarity, may choose to act or react. You have choice. No one or no thing can change or alter you or that which you are. You are the only one who can do this. You, in your totality, are given the ability to express the Divine Essence within you or not. You have choice or the use of individual will.

The vibrational pattern of the dimension holding planet Earth is being altered to allow you the opportunity to express your own divinity or come into the Christ Consciousness prior to the close of this major cycle. Please note, I have used the thought, opportunity. Each one receives regardless of dimension, and has the opportunity to use the energy vibrational pattern as they would. This alteration in vibration is not limited to your small planet, but rather has Cosmic impact.

As the vibration is experienced from the Source, so it is it can be expressed as waves or drops. Such descriptive terms merely denote the fact of a measured infusion at a specific point or space rather than a flooding. The purpose? To allow you to acclimatize to the altered vibration and grow with it. Each of you will respond to specific waves or drops in a specific manner. This too is of the Divine Purpose. All of you cannot respond at the same frequency because all of you are not at the same point in your own cycle. It would also produce such an imbalance for planet Earth and you who are with her, she would not be able to maintain her orbit or axital tilt -- something you have grown quite accustomed to. Therefore, ones will acclaim of a specific wave or drop of energy alteration because they are attuned to that wave or drop. Others will experience no thing. Their attunement will be to a different wave or drop.

Please note, what you experience. Each of you has sufficient discernment to be able to know what you feel, what you desire to be. Let no one tell you different. This is a honing and polishing of your own discernment skills. You have the ability to grow each day of your own life pattern to be all you can be. You have the ability to attain your perfection or any portion of it you desire. At this place in your own cycle, place your focus on attaining your own perfection and expressing this perfection and all will be in Divine Order.

Many terms are being used to assist you in your lessons of discernment. Do not allow yourselves to be caught up in the wave of the moment of society or of a collective consciousness, but rather focus on receiving according to your own ability and expressing from the gift you have received.

Your hour shortens, brothers and sisters. As you would say, "So little time and so much to do." We bless you even as you bless us.

About the people who have not consciously decided to make a commitment to the Light, is there still hope or time for them to decide to walk this path?

SARNA My dear ones, do not fear, for there is time until the last second...

149

Know that each one, each soul is valued according to that which it is and to that which commitment that it makes. If ones would choose the path of materialism, at this time, during this portion of your cycle, then it is their choice and it is their right. And it would be suggested that you let them be. It is that they shall enjoy re-embodiment of another cycle in a setting that is more closely tuned to one of their own vibration. No one throughout the Cosmos evolves at the same rate or the same frequency. Each soul must make its own journey. It is important that each soul be allowed to make its own journey. For if you would step forth and you would assume to hasten the journey of another soul, and this one is coming in a reluctant manner, know that you can cause a karmic condition which would work to the detriment of you or the other.

Greet each one, see of their highest virtues and let them be, even as you would be, knowing that however they evolve they are doing exactly what they should do, when they should do it.

It seems that some people are carrying specific energies. Would you give us more information about that?

KEILTA Greetings, dear ones of planet Earth. ...Indeed, all lighted ones upon the planet are transmitters and transformers, receivers, whatever word you would choose for the energies that are coming forth to Earth at this time. Most of them are acting to step down and to make the energies, or to allow the energies to be ones that are more easily absorbed by ones upon the planet.

As we speak of the Lighted ones, may I also add the thought form here, that your trees are also great transmitters and transformers of energy.

There are also ones that have come from specific galaxies, or universes that have agreed to carry specific energies for ones upon the planet until a specific time. This might even be considered as giving birth to these energies for there is a seed energy that is within specific ones. These ones have brought the energies, and here I speak on the soul level, from other universes, galaxies, and planets that they would hold these on your planet Earth until such time as it is for them to be released. At that particular time it is a birthing process for these energies are allowed to come forth, to grow, to expand that they would be available for all ones within a particular vibratory frame.

At this particular portion of your cycle on your planet Earth there are representatives from all galaxies and all universes. There are positive and negative, or as you would say wo-man and man, that are carrying seeds from each of these galaxies, universes, planets that assist or contribute to the upliftment of Earth and her inhabitants. Ones are coming into their awareness that they are carrying these seeds. As they come into this awareness, they are also aware that the seed is growing, the energy is growing within them. For it is only when it has been released from its latent stage into its active stage of development that it can be prepared to be shared with all ones upon the planet.

Mother Earth and those that are with her as they evolve into a higher dimensional consciousness and aware-ness must be able to accept the gifts of all of the rest of the Cosmos, for this is part of the movement into a higher dimen-sional state. This is the gift that is being shared by the various galaxies and universe, all portions of creation throughout the Cosmos.

Is there a significance as from where we came as to the work we are doing on Earth?

SARNA For most of you, yes. You have come from a par-ticular origin to bring a unique quality to planet Earth. Some of you have come to work with healing, to be facilitators with healing. And do not limit yourself to physical hands on healing, but recognize there are many ways that you heal.

There are those of you who have come to bring the tones of the Cosmos into sound upon your plane. There are those of you who have come to bring great color, which is then again an expression of the Divine. There are others who have come to plant seed and to bring forth and nourish the plant as it would come. And there are those who have come to assist with the systems upon your planet, those which have reached an unbalance to help them come into a balance. And there are others who have come who will work with children to bring these ones forth, up, and to help them sprout into all that they are. And there are others who have come as scholars which will anchor specific thoughts that those might be anchored for all generations upon your planet.

So these are but a few examples of the uniqueness of each of you as you have come. Your role is to know what your uniqueness is and there is much joy in that exploration.

Commander Ashtar mentioned earlier about seeking quietness. Can you give us any suggestions about meditation and setting up periods of quietness?

SARNA I am reminded of a phrase that this one (Tuieta) uses. It seems that meditation is a state that is as elusive to many of you upon your planet as is the ability for, "the cow to fly over the house". Many of you have set up this thing called meditation into something that is quite impossible, for you have placed limits upon yourself that you cannot reach. A period of quietness, a period of stillness, a period of contentment, is one in which you are allowed to receive the higher energies.

It has been suggested that you would set aside ten or fifteen minutes each day. Indeed, perhaps, two minutes each day is all that you are capable of doing at any one particular time. Recognize as you would go for your walk, or you would sit and you would gaze at the beauty of a flower, or you would feel a most glorious feeling, that this is a type of meditation. But what we are speaking of, or what we are asking of, is for that period in which you might sit yourself down quietly somewhere and you would allow the energies to come into you.

Initially, to be able to quiet your <u>active</u> mind -- and I would underscore the word active, for most of your minds are very active -- to quiet this creature, select something, a scene, an experience, something that is most pleasant to you. It might be a walk in the woods. It might be a walk by the seaside. It might be gazing at the petals of a flower. But select something that is yours that brings a joy and a peace to you. And concentrate this active mind upon this.

Initially when you do this, you may find it is but a few seconds, and that's alright. Don't push yourself. Be grateful for this few seconds of balance that you have had. And as you do this each day, you will find that your number of seconds increase. And indeed, it shall turn into minutes. And you shall find that this is a recharging time for you. It is a re-balancing time for you. And indeed, many of you that have experienced this shall find it to be quite addictive, that if you do not have your period of quietness that you get out of sorts and become quite 'crotchety', as your earth term would be.

May I initially suggest to some of you, that you would try the exercise that was given by the Master Healer from Opheus. And that is to sit comfortably, put your feet flat on the floor with your back as straight as possible and to breath in three times, each time taking in a great deep breath, recognizing as you do this you draw in the divine balanced energies within you. And as you exhale each breath, you are exhaling all of that which is not of balance, which is not of perfection. This is an exercise that might assist you initially as you would attempt to sit in a period of quietness.

This exercise also is one that those of you that are quite proficient at meditation shall find most useful to bring yourself quickly into a state of balance and harmony. For each of you as you would go out and your energies would mingle with and you would be exposed to the energies of others, find that you would enter a state of unbalance, and this exercise will assist you quite easily in coming back into your state of alignment and balance.

But to continue of those of you that are initially entering this process. Take in your breath, release the negativity and the unbalance. Again take in the breath, release the unbalances. Then concentrate your thought forms on that which is most positive to you and hold that just for a few seconds. And know that if you can do this for a few seconds, then you have done what you needed to do at that time. Do not place too high an expectation upon yourself for not everyone was meant to sit in meditation for one hour everyday. And indeed, the time that you would need for quietness will vary for each of you according to your level of attunement and your individual need at that particular time...

MONKA ...You will notice those of that which you call your eastern religions have made a practice, have made a purpose of seeking to establish their link with the Higher Source. Those of you of your western cultures have been brainwashed into the non-necessity of this. It is at this time upon your planet that ones of your western religions and your western cultures are recognizing a need for this attunement. Indeed, this practice is spreading. And while it might be called by many names the practice is the same. It is only as you regularly and consciously reach an attunement and go into the solitude that you will be able to more finely tune your own instrument, that it will vibrate more easily in a heightened frequency.

Are groups that meditate on bringing forth peace and balance helping?

JOKHYM Salutations. ...You who would gather together in

groups of two or more and your focus would be towards the upliftment of your planet and the betterment, do a great good. For indeed, by ones coming together and focusing their thoughts you have the ability to bring about a healing.

Upon this plane on which we dwell when one would be as you would say to lose a limb, we can come together and we can offer the assistance of holding the thought of the perfection of the individual that the limb would come and they would be as one whole and perfect. I use this only as an illustration.

For indeed, as you would come together in your groups and you would focus your thoughts on a specific area and you would draw in Light, the Light of the Source, so it is you are vehicles that will not only allow the Light to go to an area but you magnify it.

If I were to say to you that our job would be impossible without you, would you understand what I mean -- because it is through you that we work. You are the anchors on planet Earth that allow. You are the transformers that allow the energy to come in that it might go forth within your dimension. You may come together in a group and you may focus your energies and you can move one of the plates upon the face of your planet. You can cause the sleeping volcano to erupt if that is your choice because there is great power that you have that we might share through you. And as the Light of the Infinite One is shared through you, it is magnified and intensified that it would have a greater impact. And the greatest accelerator that it has is the purity of the motive that you have as you would assist in the healing process.

However, always, always, my children, ask that all that you do is according to Divine Will. Always ask for Divine guidance and it is according to Divine Will. And why would you have to do that? Because there are changes that will come about, there are ones that are involved in changes that are beyond your understanding, that you do not know what the reasoning is and so it is those are ones that you would not enter into.

So it is best we just try to channel energies for the highest good?

JOKHYM This is the best that you can do -- for the highest good, for the highest good of that which would receive, for those ones that would receive. Then, if you have shared for the highest good according to Divine Will then you have not trespassed on anyone else's path. You have left it open if they would desire to receive or if the planetary Mother would desire to receive. For there are certain things she must experience in order to go through her own process. But if you would say, "I would send healing because I would desire that this place in this particular part of the world is utopia on Earth", then you are placing your own expectation, you are placing your own parameters around that which you send and you are going to accept the consequences for what you have done for you are responsible for it. But if it is according to the highest good and Divine Will then you are in alignment with the Divine One.

What about our own will and that of Divine Will?

SARNA ...Even as you have that which is free will, you could say this is a way of working with that which you have been given which is called an ego, because is not free will an instrument of ego? And it is only as you would say, "Thy Will, not mine," that you would desire an alignment.

And ones would say, "You would give up your will?" And ones would say, "The only way you make progress is to give up your will." You do not give up your will -- you align your will with that which is the Total.

You would say this is a game of words. It is not a

game of words. It is important that you understand the difference in the two concepts. For one means you are entering into a subservient position. The other means you are aligning and coming into oneness. And that is the difference.

When one has thoughts that are unbalancing what is suggested as the best, fastest, efficient way to regain ones focus?

MONKA The first is the desire to shift the focus, and the second is the action, and the third is the result of the action -- which is the shift in focus. But it must always be initiated by that which is desire -- honest desire in truth...

Now, I will add a thought. You cannot shift another's focus, you know. But each must do that which is theirs according to their own path. And you are in a place of your cycle where there are many parting and there are many going in various directions. And it would seem there are those who have focused on what you are sure is not right for them. Perhaps the lesson there is to release them, for you cannot guide another's focus. It must be a desire from within. And those of you who would desire to play at games shall find you are falling by the wayside, for this is truly the time that the warrior is donning their armor. You are rolling up your sleeves and you are finding there are many ways you are becoming very active and very busy. Is this not so?

Can you give us any assistance on how to release a thought; to release, and to know it is released, that is, letting go?

MONKA Every time it comes to you, replace it with the desired thought. Bless it and release it. Bless it and release it -- for has it not served a great purpose? And as you bless it and release it it shall come to you less frequently. But perhaps it has not had its blessing yet, is the reason it keeps returning. As you will continue to do this, and because you are on a plane of imperfection, imperfection will stay with you more easily. So it is a double opportunity, to bless and release and re-focus. Can you do that? Work, and we will assist you.

The purpose of this particular cycle in which we are in this dimension, is it partially one of duality, of will, of physicality? How do these things interrelate as to what we are attempting to achieve in, not this embodiment, but this whole process of our evolution here on this plane? And how do the things such as will, physicality, fit into a graduation process as we see it in this particular plane in which we are? And what does graduation mean?

JOKHYM ....Your physicality, your form, merely has to do with the vibrational pattern in which you are functioning... If you will get caught up in the dimensional vibration you are in, you will be caught up in that which is physicality. You will be placed in a position where always you are in a duality situation, not recognizing why the duality...

If you have maintained and you desire to maintain a communicative link with that which is beyond your dimension, you will see your physicality for what it is. It is merely a vehicle which operates at a specific vibrational pattern in which your divinity functions. That also allows you the awareness of why the experience. That experience is the execution of Divine Will bringing forth that essence of Creation, of Creator. So it is according to your level of functioning within your dimension -- and level is not a good word -- shall we say, your awareness of functioning within your dimension as to how you will see or experience the whole experience.

So if you acknowledge only the duality, then that is what you will experience. If you acknowledge only the physicality of your being, then that is what you experience.

But if you would integrate and begin to put together thoughts which come to you, you will see there is that which encompasses the total vibration, and that is the introduction and the introspection and the integration of Divine Will within a specific vibration...

(Regarding graduation) You look at graduation in a duality sense. You look at it as either fail or pass. And it is neither; it is neither. It is simply that you as an individual have achieved a specific vibration, a specific understanding if you will. And if you do this, then it means you enter into that which is a vibration which will allow you a greater expansion. But because of your duality programming, it is either a pass or a fail. It is either an up or a down. And it is neither.

You have been in a cycle, and your cycle, your grand cycle, is coming to a close. Many of you have been ones who have been with other planetary systems, if you will; other planets, other places, and you signed on for a cycle. Now if during this cycle you have, shall we say, grown in your own awareness, you then have the opportunity not to have to go through the experiences of that growth cycle again. But you would then go perhaps to what you would call Earth in her newness, or you would return home, whatever. But you would bring an expanded awareness and consciousness wherever you are. Now if you were one who did not want to expand in your consciousness, then it's quite simple: You wouldn't have to go through that experience. It is all a growth process. It is not a growth process, but it is a growth process...

You recognize of the close or the finish of this particular opportunity for a specific growth pattern. You have had this pattern to introduce, introspect, and integrate Divine Will within all of the essences which are within you. Now, if you have not done that, then you will have opportunity again for Divine Will, but it will also be in conjunction with another essence. This is part of the process which goes on and on and on...

If you will grow within your own selves, you can learn to work with the Law of Attraction within your dimension. And through that Law of Attraction you may attract to you, all that you need. No, you will not manifest it, but you will attract it from the dimensional vibration which you are in.

And if you are guided that you would put up stores, then follow that which is your individual guidance. If you are guided that you would collect sheets of music, then do so. Follow your own guidance. The hour of doing something en masse is long past, because you are not a mass consciousness. You are individual entities, and you are divine.

What is the worst thing that can happen to you in your estimation? It would be that your form would get hurt in some way, is it not? But your form is not eternal. Even if you would have that which you would call physical liftoff, when you got there you wouldn't like your form; you'd want to get rid of it. This has been the experience in the past of ones that have been picked up. They haven't liked their form. They have wanted to get rid of it once they have gotten with us.

If you will recognize of the divinity within you, then all else falls in place and you don't have to be concerned about soups; you don't have to be concerned about wheat berries; you don't have to be concerned about holidays or how much monies you have in the bank, because you attract to you where your focus is. That is part of your dimension; that is the Law of Attraction. You attract what you put out. And if you would feel in this total process that you are going to go under, then that is exactly what you will attract to you.

If you can, one, recognize you are eternal, you are immortal -- whatever word you would use -- I would choose to say you are divine; and recognize that you have within your dimension that which is the Law of Attraction and that Law of Attraction says, whatever you desire, what thoughts you put out, you can attract it to you. Was it not said to you, you could feed the masses by merely sharing the thought

160

with them that they would share of the energy of your bread? This puts into action the Law of Attraction in two ways: Because you are sharing, the energy which you are sharing begins to be experienced through these ones, and also, because this is happening they attract to them that which is the earthly bread. Begin to work with these things.

I would sound perhaps as I am being impatient, and I am, I will not deny that, because you look at yourselves and you see your being. You see your houses; you see what's in your cupboard or what's not in your cupboard. You see your vehicles as you would ride around in them. And this is how you define yourself. I don't see that at all. What I see is the energy of your divinity and the energy pattern which you are, and it is asking to come into a clarity, into a brightness, shall we say. And all you're doing by getting tied up with these things is, you're making it more cloudy.

Could you tell us more about the Law of Attraction and drawing experiences to us?

JOKHYM What you are doing is you are coming into an awareness of the Law of Attraction that you are drawing to you that which you need for balance, or shall we say to try to attain balance. If you could close your eyes and you would see yourself as an energy vibration that is constantly moving and changing, then you would look at each one beside you and you would see that they are doing also this. And this vibration that you are is seeking a more fine attunement within your dimension. And so it is it would see from this relationship perhaps an opportunity for attunement that is finer. And even that is an erroneous thought because when I say "finer," it is not grander, it is a finer vibration.

And so it is that by doing this, you are taking the energies, you are drawing the energies to you to assist you in this balancing process because you are an energy vibration, that you are vibrating at a specific density even as that wall is vibrating at a specific density, even as this one vibrates; and your flower. Each is at its own particular vibration to produce a specific density. And you draw to you from within that vibrational frequency the energies to assist you in your balancing. That is the Law of Attraction.

Now you can do this without consciously doing this, or you may begin to focus yourself, your thinking, your emotions, your physical, to focus your totality and draw to you that which you desire. That is then the conscious portion of the Law of Attraction -- for you attract whether you want to admit it or not...

Look at what comes to you. Each of you, as you would have a situation within your own life stream and it would be that which would be a most unique situation, shall we say, take a few moments and look and say, "How did I attract this? What did I do? What was there about me that attracted that?" And one of you might say, "Oh, I didn't do anything." Yes, there was something about you that attracted the situation. But you just must go deep enough that you find it, what it is that has attracted it. But you can consciously focus and attract to you as you desire. This is coming into the steps of mastery.

This one that is known to you as the Master Jesus, this he did. He was in command of the Law of Attraction. And, he could bring together by his own interaction with that within the dimension, as he so desired.

Did he attract the experience of the crucifixion to him?

JOKHYM He attracted this. He knew that he was not to live for a ripe old age, shall we say, upon your plane, because the teachings and the seeds of the teachings that he would bring forth had greater impact by intensity rather than duration. The intensity would stay him through the ages. There was also that which was most difficult and has had no recording within your books: For one to maintain the vibrational frequency of the Christed energies for an extended period upon your planet is indeed most difficult on the form that it would inhabit.

And so it was this crucifixion that you speak of, had several, shall we say, positive aspects to it. For it allowed ones to see of this public humiliation from your plane which was totally unacceptable to the masses, to see that this one was not limited by that, but indeed demonstrate to you the eternalness that you are. And so it was the purpose was served.

And it was not that he died for your sins. For you this sin situation has gotten totally out of hand upon your planet. If you would say there is a "sin", there is but one sin and that is to deny the divinity that you are and the divinity that Is. That is the only "sin" if you would use such a word. And what does that do? In that denial you attract only that which is your separateness from that which is the divinity that you are in the Source Of All Being...

It was mentioned earlier about searching within. Presumably this will help us receive guidance, and if so how do we know we can trust this guidance when we get it?

HATONN Greetings, dear ones. ...Do each of you remember when you were a small child and you got on the two-wheeled mechanism that you called a bicycle, and you had seen others as they would zip past you on these two wheels, and you were small and you longed to do this also? And so it was that you got up on this contraption, and if you were fortunate there was a parent, an older brother, an older sister, who would help steady your bicycle for you when you would start out. Gradually they would run beside you or behind you until finally you were going off down your roadway and you were doing very well. Until it dawned on you that they were no longer holding onto the back of the bicycle. And then you stopped. Most often you fell. Then you would pick yourself up and again you would go through this same experience. Only this time when you realized that they were no longer holding to your bicycle, you knew it was alright to go on, that you had been riding on your own, you had been peddling your own bicycle. So it is the lessons that are given to you. They are as the stability for your bicycle.

The first thing that must be there is the desire. This you have. The next is the practice. For always as you would go forth the older brother would be there to assist you, or ones who have already learned how to ride down this particular path. So you must allow yourself to go. You must allow yourself to take the initiation, the initial steps, knowing that sometimes the initial guidance may not be as accurate as you would desire. But there is a check system within you, that should the information that manifests within you not be as complete as would be best for you, there would be a question within you as to it. In that case, wait.

Three times, in three different ways, you will get confirmation, each of you. Your confirmation may come from the shared thought of another, it may come as a vision, it may be something that you would read within your newspaper or see upon your television screen. But your confirmation will come, particularly when you first start peddling on your own. And know that if you are not comfortable with this, and you begin to wobble, that there will always be one of the elder ones there to hold on to the back of your seat to help to steady you.

Please speak on any special significance at the time of the equinoxes, solstices, full moon and new moon. How do these times effect us physically, mentally, emotionally and spiritually?

SARNA ...At the time of that which is known as your solstice, the four of them within your calender year, these are specific

164

times, to use your earthean phrase, that energies are intro-duced into the ethers of Earth. Gradually, ever so gradually, through the evolutionary process upon your planet at these four periods, energies have been introduced to assist in rais-ing the vibratory frequency of Mother Earth and those that dwell with her. Recognize that there are no new energies that are introduced -- even though we use this term. It is an inaccuratism. But it is merely that energies are brought forth in an attunement and notice is given for your awareness.

Your physical vehicle, your brain, your consciousness, your emotional state all react to that which is introduced. In some instances the energies are ones that cause an unset-tling within you. In other instances they are as a soothing balm for you. Each is given to assist in your evolution and in elevating your own awareness in your soul's progression.

These energies as they come also effect the air about you, your food, your planet. They effect all that you are aware of on your conscious plane, plus more.

At specific times, specific energies are introduced. Those that you are approaching (spring) are known as the awakening energies. These are as the ones of the union of the male and the female, the positive and the negative. These are the creative energies that come forth to you each year at this period. Those that come forth to you at your summer solstice are those that bring forth the growth ener-gies...

At the time which is known as your fall [equinox] this is a time of unsettling, for many ones of the dark robes are given license within the Plan to attempt to woo ones over. This is a cleansing and a sorting process to make each of you ready for the Christed energies that enter in your winter solstice. As all else about your planet would prepare to sleep, so it is the Divine Christed energies come forth that they would then trigger the positive and negative in your spring time, your summer growth, your fall cleansing. And so the cycle goes.

As each of these cycles or mini cycles is completed, you react to these energies in your own individual way according to where you are in your own evolvement. Some of you may experience tears. You may find that you are emotionally quite unstable. And those of you that perchance work with your hospitals may notice an increase in the number of admissions. There are those times when you physically react to the energies that are coming forth. Some of you may experience various aches and pains of your vehicle as well as unbalances within your organs.

At this particular time of your cycle, and here I am speaking of the greater cosmic cycle rather than that which you know as a yearly cycle, the energies are introduced at specific times upon the planet as we have discussed, and yet there is a heightened push, a finer attunement, a finer vibration that is coming to you as each set of energies is introduced. There is not the slacking off period that you were afforded before you reached the end of your cycle and the beginning of the next one. This is a constant manifestation for you. This is done in an attempt to assist all of you to make your choices consciously, to bring your total being into alignment, and to manifest the highest that you can manifest within your present embodiment. This is part of being at the end of one cycle and the beginning of the next.

We recognize that many of you are experiencing many manifestations because of these energy patterns. And in your sleep state we work with you most closely to assist you in maintaining a measure of balance as the energies come in and those that are about you go forth, and there is conflict in this. We would assist in helping you in your attunement. I trust this has answered your question, and has also caused a bit of curiosity to stir also.

* * * * *

This has been a rather intense discussion, has it not? Let us now close. Each may now return to their private abode whether it be on Earth or elsewhere. Sarna, out.

HELPING OTHERS

Good evening. I trust everyone is centered and ready to begin this portion of the discussions. Tonight, we will speak on the topic of helping others. Cuptan Fetogia as well as Lord Dionus, Commanders Beatrix, Jokhym, Monka, and Hatonn and Captain Keilta and I will answer questions and share thoughts. You may begin your questions.

I find it very difficult to understand what I can do for the planet and for myself and the people around me. How do we find our purpose and survive materially, financially, and to be able to love and give? Sometimes I get so frustrated in not knowing, that sometimes I don't want to be here.

BEATRIX Greetings, dear ones. ...It is a very good question that you ask, for that which you have expressed is expressed by each of you in one way or another at some point in your own evolution.

You exist. You do your job. You go to your place of toil. You take care of whatever it is you take care of. And you would say, "Is there nothing better? Do I not have a greater purpose than this?" The purpose is to learn yourself and to be able to glean for yourself balance out of the unbalance. For indeed, you are in a vibrational pattern that is unbalanced. As you grow in your balance, you find your awareness expands.

You have heard frequently of that which is called new eyes or a new vision. It does not mean that you don't need bifocals, it merely means that you see things with different eyes. The energy you put into what you are doing is a different energy because you can see purpose in what you are doing. You can put a portion of your vibration in whatever you do. Even if it would be that which is called getting upon your conveyances, your buses, can you not give your seat to one who can't stand as easily as you? Or could you perhaps carry the bag for one who has too many things to carry? Or there is one who has a small child, could you perhaps lift this one off and on the conveyance? And can you smile at your brother? Can you look them in the eye as you would walk down your roads, your streets. Can you look them in the eye and smile?

You will find as you walk down your street there are many ones whose gaze will not meet yours for it is down. And even if they see you look at them, they will look away. But as you would look one in the eye and you would smile at them, you are acknowledging them and all of the worth that they are.

There are many ones upon your plane who would ask for great and mighty missions and purpose. The greatest purpose anyone can have is to first be all you can be. Be this in preparing your food for your family. When you prepare it, put love in it. Do it in a loving manner. When you would put your children to sleep and put them in their bed, do this with love in your heart. When you would clean your house, your dwelling place, recognize that this is your sanctuary, that you want no negative vibration to be there, so let it be a joyful act. And when you would clothe your temple, clothe it that it reflects the beauty that you are that others might see of this and know of your own beauty.

You do not have to stand on your street corners and beat drums. You do not have to carry great reams of pamphlets to others. But you can be all you can be each day. So when you would prepare for slumber, you would be able to commune with your Source and say, "I tried. I did the best that I could today." Or perhaps there would be a day when you would say, in this ones jargon, "I blew it. And tomorrow I'll try again."

But the purpose is to become the god that you are and as you do this, so it is you help all others to do it also.

There are times I feel really wiped out by ones who seem to drain energy from me. Is there anything that you can share along that line and how can we be aware of these ones?

JOKHYM Salutations, dear ones. ...If you would for a moment picture a sponge... Now see this sponge, and shall we for the sake of our example, see a nice round rosy pink sponge, and see this one that it is filled to the point that it is, yes, drippy. And as it drips we shall give legs to this sponge as it walks about. And as it drips so is this precious liquid that fills it left where ever it has gone. And so is the air about it and around it receiving the energies, the liquid, the water, the life that is within the sponge. Now if our sponge receives no more water, what happens? It dries up, it becomes quite hard, and it is cast away, is this not so?

Now, for a moment if you would please, see this sponge again that is filled, for as it loses of its liquid and it becomes dry and it is again placed in liquid it grows fat and round and squashy, and begins to drip as it goes forth.

And now behold here is... (another) sponge and it is dry. It is as a board it is so dry, and it is hard. And here you come all drippy and wet. And you go forth. And, aha, there is moisture that is emitted from this sponge, and the moisture that goes from this sponge touches the dry sponge. And the dry sponge is no longer as dry, and it feels of this, and it is a much more pleasant feeling. It is much more comfortable than this dry, hard, crackly state. And so this dry sponge as it receives of the moisture laps it up. And it goes over closer to you, our beloved soppy sponge, and it gathers of your liquid. And so what happens? You both become partially wet, but you are both partially dry.

Now recognize that this is a most elementary example that I have given to you. But in essence, from an energy point of view in many instances, this is what happens to ones of Earth. For there are ones on Earth, both from the outward minds eye and from the higher, from the soul area, that are indeed hungry, that need energies to survive.

Shall we speak briefly of the soul that is trying most desperately to reach a balance with the being and with the mind. This one needs all the nourishment that it can get as it tries so desperately to bring forth this balance. It cannot gather its sustenance from its mind, from its being. And though the higher energies come it cannot receive in sufficient quantity that it might come forth to be in balance and harmony, for there is a blockage from the mind and from the being.

Now you who have opened up, who are our transformers, who have stored of the energies come in contact with ones such as this, and you are easy energies. That which you have is easily acceptable. Shall we say the energies that are within you are as the baby foods for they are easily digested by the soul of the other. And so it is you feel zapped, to use your earthly terms. For this one is most appreciative that you would feed it, this soul is. It is most grateful for it hungers and you willingly -- now you must remember this, you do this willingly -- you share of your energies with this other one.

Now this is done on an unconscious level by this other one, this dry sponge that we had talked of earlier. There are also, ones that consciously feel, that consciously attempt to take from you that which you would freely share. These are ones that their minds eye says, "I need that which this one has." And they are as ones that would take a straw, and they would drink the liquid from the sponge. These ones that are known upon your plane as vampires are not always ones that would take of the blood of another, so much as they would sap the life blood, the energy flow, that comes from another. This is the true vampire. And so it is that you have two types of individuals that accept that which you freely share.

...If you are going into a situation where you feel that you might be vulnerable do as the Lord Michael says, call forth the blue flame, the mighty blue flame from the sword of the Lord Michael that it might surround you once, twice, thrice. So be it. It is done. So says the blessed Lord Michael. Do this to your being. If my calculation is correct, on the earthly terms, this should take you approximately two and one-half of your seconds. Not much time would you say?

And then recognize that the majority of the energy that goes through you to another goes out from your solar plexus area. As you protect yourself with your hands with this symbol of protection (folding arms in front of you), recognize that you do this in front of your solar plexus area. And of course, you have been told of the violet flame as well as the flame of protection. You know of the ability of the beautiful amethyst to transmute energies. Call upon this that you also might be protected in this area. And say to yourself, declare for yourself, that you are a total being, that you are a manifestation of the Godhead upon this plane, and naught but that which you would freely give shall go from you. And naught but that which you would freely receive shall come to you. Make your declaration.

How can we help those who do not believe in life beyond this planet?

JOKHYM ...Obviously, it would be most disconcerting for many ones on your planet if you were to begin your conversation with, "The brothers of space tell me, such and such." Indeed, this might limit your audience quite abruptly, would it not in most instances? Yet, some of you have tried this tactic and it has worked quite well with a select few, a select few, for they were as ones ready to hear of this little phrase. But what of these ones that are about you? And we will speak of that which is your work place, those that you would meet in your market, those that you would meet at your organizations, etc. What of these ones?

Most that you know would know that you are one of those that is different, perhaps, than your brethren, in that your thinking has followed a path that is not acceptable by the greater masses at this time. And so, as ones would come to you and they would say, "What is happening?" Perhaps you might reply with, "What do you think is happening? What do you feel? What do you experience? What are your thoughts?" And as you would do this then you would allow the other one to bring into a conscious awareness state, a formulation of what they are experiencing themselves. Thus, this will give you a base from which to begin to talk.

Recognize that love is universal, and unfortunately, or fortunately, whichever you would choose to use, you do not have the corner on the market, but love has been felt throughout and about your planet for eons. It is that the level and attunement of love which we speak is one that has not been familiar. But to speak of love of brother, love of Earth, a desire that Earth not be destroyed, a desire to be at-one-ness with your Creator Source, these are not new thoughts. Could you pose the question that perhaps there are experiences, there are energies, there are cycles? Cycles are not a term that are foreign to most ones. Indeed, oft you will hear ones mention, "Things go in cycles. There will be a full turn of the cycle and such and such will return to you." So this thought of cycle is not a foreign one. This might be a stepping off point to speak of as ones would ask what is happening.

And you find out what they are experiencing. Perhaps they are experiencing no physical imbalances, they merely have a yearning within themselves and they do not understand it. But know they have been attracted to you to bring up this topic. They have sought you out to speak of these things, so there is a kinship because they have sought you out and they have spoken of this. I would underscore: Just as we have done with you upon your planet, begin your

172

<u>lessons, your teachings, where the student is.</u> If the student has no difficulty with speaking of brethren and silver ships, then so be it, may you speak of this. But if this is frightening or the idea that ones might come in and they would speak through another and this causes a great disharmony within the individual, then perhaps this is not the approach to take. Begin where the student is. That is lesson one.

The second lesson is: Do not give the student too much, but always let the student lead you with a hunger to know more.

Lesson three: Perhaps you might easily end your discussion with a question that the other might ponder.

Lesson four: Let your initial discussions be most brief and always framed within the frame of reference of the student.

Lesson five: Express by your manner, in truth, that you have a universal love of this one and regardless of whether they would choose to pursue the topic or not, this love for them is not altered, for this is allowing them to be where they need to be.

Lesson six: If the student does not choose to pursue the topic, do not chase them down the alley. Light workers are notorious for this. Indeed, it would be that you put on roller skates in your chase, or perhaps, in desperation, you would execute a perfect tackle for you are convinced that it is the path for you as it should be the path for all ones. So let this one walk at their own pace.

Lesson seven: As the initial comments are ones of brevity, as the student is ready, share longer discussions.

Lesson eight: Do not load the student down with great stacks of books. Most ones of the Light have been ones that have sought and they have read on their own and they have been as ones hungry to read that they might have a greater understanding. Do not weigh another down but let them inquire according to where they are. Guide their steps that they might make their own selections, for you must recognize that which has assisted you may not be the assistor of another.

Lesson nine: Recognize that you cannot be teacher for all ones, but each has a unique gift that might be shared with a specific group of entities. Should an entity not respond, then so be it. Let them be. But you have not failed because you have not converted every one in your city.

And lesson ten: Know that you have direct guidance as you would share with others. You have but to be in a state of balance, and this will become obvious to you.

Now, this has been a capsule approach that you might use with ones that are stirring. Please note that I did not use the term, awakening, but rather, they are stirring. It is up to you to give them the crumb that will spark the desire for the awakening. Most all ones upon your planet have had some type of experience that they cannot explain. And as you would get into discussions of that which is beyond your dimensional understanding or your dimensional manifestation, so it is that they would share these with you.

In your most learned manner, may I suggest to you, perhaps, lesson eleven: Do not become the authority on another's unexplained experience, for indeed, your interpretation might create a barrier for future growth for either one of you. There is much that has happened and is happening upon your planet that is not explainable within the known assimilation brought in by your five senses. And ones are becoming eager to share these experiences, for indeed, there has been sufficient publicity on your media that allows ones to do this...

Is there anything that we can do within Divine Order when we see people that are suffering?

SARNA The first thing that you might do is bless these ones.

Recognize that they have taken on a portion of this suffering as their method of evolving, or that they might assist others in their own evolution.

This is a lesson that is very difficult for you upon your planet. You would see the beggar and your heart would ache that you would bring him to your door and you would feed him and you would clothe him. And then you would let him go through your door to again assume the position of beggar that he was in before. For though you have felt a great pity for one you have not felt a binding love in brotherhood.

There are ones upon your planet that have come and they experience great suffering. For they assume part of the suffering of Mother Earth as well as part of the suffering of mankind. Love these ones and allow them to be. Assist as you might assist, that you would serve with them that you would create no servitude on your part or theirs, and let them be. Love these ones as brothers, as sisters. Love them sufficiently that you would let them suffer. That you would ease their pain, that is your role, but always, always ask for divine guidance in all that you do, that you would create no karma for you, or for them. Because the veil has fallen for most of you at this time, you do not recognize much of that which is transpiring for your brother. So it is that you must always ask for guidance in this direction before you proceed -- recognizing there have been some that have come that do suffer to allow you the opportunity to assist him. Each is on a most individual basis. And I would urge you to always ask for guidance as to how you would proceed...

How do we know where to find the "line" when we're trying to help another?

MONKA Greetings, beloveds. ...Is your back tired? ("Yes.") Then you've stepped over the line, for one is riding upon it. When you're back is weary you know you have stepped over the line. One of the greatest, most difficult feats there is for you upon your plane is to love someone so much you release them totally. And it is most painful for you. And I know that pain because there are ones upon your planet whom I have released from mine, and I did not want to let them go. But I knew I must, for their own growth.

For if you're back is weary, you know you are carrying another, and perhaps they are too big to be carried and they should stand on their own feet. And perhaps this is what must be told to them. And then you add, "I will hold forth my hand that you would walk beside me, but I will not carry you. I ask you to walk beside me." And every time your back gets weary, see who is sitting there.

How many of you, you have sore shoulders and backs? Who are you carrying? What are you carrying? Through the eyes through which I see at this moment, I see great boulders for some of you. It's a wonder you can stand at all. It is called the weight of the world, hmm? Release it, and let the world come and walk with you...

I am not sure I totally understand. Can you give us an example? For instance, when we watched the Los Angeles riots on television, how could we help the people involved?

MONKA When you would look at that which is your screen and there would be any instance of unbalance, immediately see it in balance.

Take that which is the situation in which there was ones who were pulled from their car or they were beaten. Do you remember that scene? See that, not as ones being pulled from their car or beaten, but you see that as ones who are helping these ones through the situation, and the ones in the car can open their doors to let others ride that need to ride. See brother in harmony with brother; and that is asking a lot, is it not? But you can do this with practice.

But where do we cross the line of interfering with their free will, or are you just suggesting we send love to the situation in different words?

MONKA You are seeing the situation in balance. What you are doing is, you are not looking at the situation which you see on your screen, but you are looking at that which is called the Christ consciousness of the situation, and you are dealing with it -- not on the individual situation that you see -- but you are dealing with it on a different level, which is the Christ consciousness level, because on that level there is only that which is perfection. But if you choose to remain in that which you see on your box and there is one who would lift their hand against another, and you would say, "Oh, no, I don't see that," you are changing what is happening there between two individuals and you're interfering with free will. But if you will... work with that which is the Christ consciousness which is just above the entity. Do you get the difference? It is important that you understand the difference, because you are shifting from your third dimension, fourth dimension, to your thirteenth. And it takes a quick trip...

Could you talk more about the question of some of us taking on karma for others?

JOKHYM ...Many ones have come as families upon the planet at this particular place in your evolutionary cycle. And I will give this to you as an illustration. Say there is a family that has come, and there are five parts to that family. The sixth part remains in the ethers and does not take on a physical form; however, the other five portions do.

There is work that is needed in a particular place upon the planet. The soul that has embodied in that particular place must get on with it. Hence, there would be that which would be another one of the family that would take on certain karmic patterns for the total family. This would free up this other one to do specific work that must be done. In turn, as there would be other embodiments, these activities by the total family would be known and would be observed. Hence, there was a balancing in the family, that the whole family evolved. This was agreed to prior to the embodiments...

Can spiritual growth and understanding be determined by a group consciousness?

KEILTA Greetings, dear ones of planet Earth. ...Your growth is an individual one. You cannot effect the growth of another, and yet you have great impact upon the growth of another if you recognize and understand the interrelationship of one being with another. However, your greatest service for all ones upon your planet is for you to come forth in your own perfection and to manifest the God essence which is within you. As you do this, so you assist others in also doing this.

The collective consciousness of Earth Mankind began with the first thought of the first being upon the planet. It is an accumulation of all thoughts which have come forth from all consciousnesses, all levels of consciousness connected with planet Earth. It has impact upon you as an entity who is within the vibration of Earth.

You as an individual, who would desire to achieve your highest, has great impact upon the collective consciousness. You as an individual do not have to be governed by the collective consciousness, but as long as you operate within a single dimension, then you are affected by the consciousness of that dimension.

It would appear that I am contradicting myself, but I am not...

We have been told that as individuals we are making great strides in our spiritual progression, but as a society in general we are kind of slow in making the changes needed for the Earth right now. So the ques-

tion is, where is it that humanity's collectiveness is lacking to take those giant steps?

MONKA The largest gap, if you will, is that which is between the soul and its expression within the individual. Each one upon planet Earth, the Emerauld, is an entity of balanced expression translated by you as a loving entity who respects all life forms. However, this knowledge has been slow to come into the consciousness of the majority. For eons upon your planet man has sought to control and manipulate his fellow man. This continued manipulation has been one for power. And unfortunately many ones have been willing to give their power to others, and others have willingly accepted it. This has placed an imbalance on the individual evolvement as well as the evolvement of the collective.

When man can see the relationship of brother with man in all others and all kingdoms on your planet, this will then be that which you would call the quantum leap. You who are the workers of the Light are assisting the total consciousness to stir and grow. For this, we thank you.

Why do we have gatherings of Light workers? What purpose do they really serve?

CUPTAN FETOGIA Salutations, Eartheons. ...Specific functions or gatherings of ones are being established upon the planet. Specific gatherings are being implemented upon your planet to bring about an activation of specific energy centers or vortexes upon the planet. These gatherings are being orchestrated by those of us within the (Inner Council) Ring to bring about the gathering of eagles and angels that have committed themselves to the upliftment of the planet, and to bring about the marriage of the evolutionary path of those with the Emerauld with those of the other dimensions, universes, and galaxies.

This that has been the school is now being brought

into a new vibration. These ones that are called to specific gatherings are coming together to anchor and to ground specific energy patterns to assist in the stabilization of all of planet Earth.

The numbers of ones who have come as the bearers of Light has not been as high as they were at the time of the initial steps of entering into this particular service. We recognize that many ones have succumbed to that which is the density of the plane; however, as these gatherings manifest upon the planet they shall bring forth the anchoring of the energies to assist in the propulsion of Earth into a dimension of multiple exposure and involvement as well as evolvement...

Do these gatherings increase the amount of Light that is anchored on Earth?

DIONUS Salutations, Eartheans. ...The activities of Earth man have been reviewed by that which is known to you as your Hierarchy, as well as by those of us of the Confederation. Setting aside specific events, the general flow of Light from this your planet called Earth, has not appreciably increased. However, there have been specific times, specific events, that have caused a great heightening in the amount of love that has flowed from the hearts of ones upon the planet -- such as your gatherings for peace, the time of the Convergence, and indeed, the hour when the treaty was signed between the two major countries upon your planet. At these times, the overall outpouring has shown a significant increase; however, this has not been of the nature to show radical alterations in the Light patterns emitted from Earth.

As you are aware, there have been some specific geophysical changes that have manifested for you, as well as those changes that were brought about by the actions of man upon your planet... At such times that there were specific geophysical changes, there was a great outpouring once again of the love, the Light, from one part of your planet to another. However, this has not been maintained in the everyday life routines of most ones upon the planet. However, as these particular times have shown a markedly increase, that, in combination with the energies that have been introduced to your planet at this particular time of your calendar year (Christmas season), have caused a slight -- and I would emphasize the word slight, for indeed it is not a great shift -- in the axis tilt of your planet. For indeed, you have righted yourselves, shall we say, one millisecond of one degree. Many of you experienced or noted specific physical changes within your form as you experienced this axital shift.

Sometimes, when I am in a circle or a gathering, I feel strong energies. I would like to be able to utilize these as I go forth. How can I do this?

HATONN Greetings, dear ones. ...As you sit within this (gathering), and as we send forth the energies, and the energies that emit from your being come forth and they mingle one with another and with those that are shared so are each of you as a sponge that you soak these up. For this is the purpose. It is intended that you would soak these up, that you would feel full, satisfied to the point that you might even be a might drippy. And so it is that you gather in these. And as you go forth -- as you know from our analogy of the sponge -- that as the sponge is held to the atmosphere so does the liquid that was in the sponge evaporate and go forth from it. And so it is that from your most precious being that which you have received goes forth to all those that touch your path, that it also sustains you in your period as you leave of this circle, of this companionship, that you are nourished. Your being is nourished, it is balanced, it is fed, and there is ample shared with you that it goes forth to be shared with others.

Recognize that this is not always a conscious sharing on your part, but much is done on a level that is higher than your conscious recognition. This is brought to your attention that you might consciously know this is what you are doing. And as you enter a particular situation, and you would call forth the energies that are stored within your being to be shared with ones so shall you also feel the flooding as additional energies are shared with you to fill your cup to overflowing.

Each of you, my brethren, are transformers to share that which you receive. For I assure you, you are not of the selfish vein that you would be as ones to lap up that which is given with no thought of sharing it with another. For if you were bent towards this direction you would not be comfortable to sit in our circle.

* * * * *

The subject of helping others is one which stirs much in the hearts of all of us. After all, none of us would be in the positions we are in if we did not carry a strong desire of this nature. However, it is very difficult for us to understand that the greatest assistance we can be is to grow in our own connection with the God Essence and bring that into beingness.

Go forth in joy, knowing you have locked within yourself a very special purpose for your existence and expression.

Sarna, out.

TOOLS

Good evening. Once again our group grows as we speak more and more of topics which are close to your hearts, those which offer assistance for you in the troubled times on Earth. This evening we will speak of the topic "tools" to assist you. Our leaders for the discussions will be Commanders Ashtar, Athena, Monka, Hatonn, Beatrix, Emartus, Jokhym, and Captain Keilta and I. Commander Ashtar will begin the discussion.

* * * * *

Ashtar here. Blessings in the Light of the Radiant One.

As you are aware, I have been rather specific in my communiques with you in your recent times. At this point, I would like to discuss the use of tools for ones spiritual elevation.

Tools are observed by us in use by many ones. One point in your history was one in which these facilitated the alteration in energy vibration which assisted ones to rise spiritually in their own. There was also a period in which the ones of the accepted religions hawked the use of specific tools as assistors to put monies in the coffers. The masses were used to support the few. The masses in their unknowing bought these tools in blind faith believing them to be of benefit. That time frame is no longer present.

The introduction of the energy vibration from the Son/Sun Station at your Christ-Mass period in the late of your year 1988 was an introduction of energies specifically for the acceleration of the consciousness of man. It was not a vibration alteration which would infuse tools or the Earth Mother.

Man goes through various stages in his personal recognition of his own divine qualities. One of these stages is the use of tools which also includes specific locations for his own spiritual advancement.

What are these tools? A tool is anything which is external from the totality of the individual. A tool is anything which man attributes to having power beyond his own. A tool is an assistor in its highest use. A tool is oft times that to which man gives power when he cannot recognize of his own divinity. A tool is just that, a tool. It cannot change your life pattern. It cannot give you information you do not already have. It cannot lead you to the divinity you are. A tool cannot give you specific gifts. It can only assist you in seeing the already known to you.

Earth mankinds has truly given much of his own power over to crystals, rods, gems, potions and such. He has worked most diligently in developing the skill and ability to use these for the highest good, while he has not put forth the time and energy in developing his own gifts to produce the same effect. He has paralyzed himself for the sake of a tool.

May I, with your indulgence, speak here of specific geographical locations. There are areas on your planet which hold a particular significance historically for specific ones. There are specific areas on your planet which hold specific vibrations. There are areas on your planet which hold specific mysteries. However, man has flocked to locations without waiting for his own inner guidance to tell him if the journey is for his benefit. He has entered an area and been "awed" by the experience. Yet, he has not truly been led to go there or to experience. He has merely experienced an anticipated alteration in energy vibration. He has bought into the "barking" of others as to his own experience and indeed, his own need.

He has not stayed in his own place, experienced the quietness and oneness with the nature mother or the family relationship of all that is around him. He has followed the suggestions of others as to what he is to experience, where he is to experience it and how he is to relate to the experience. He has been eager to be led about, accepting what others tell him to expect.

We hear many ones at this point asking for specific location geographically. We cannot repeat too often, to listen to the still voice within yourself. Recognize you have chosen to reside in a particular place by your own guidance. What are the gifts which are readily available for you in that particular place? Do not be in such a hurry to relocate that you do not experience all the experiences necessary for your present place. Are you guided to go to a place for your own external enjoyment or for your own personal growth? Let you lead you.

This is the period in which each must stand as the individual deity which they are, turning away from the "hype" and "barking" of the vendor who would seek to make a profit off you. This is the period which you can cast aside your tools, your travels, to sit quietly with yourself. Let the guidance which is yours individually lead you to your own Son/Sun energies. Feel them expand within your own being. Stand in the Light which you are. See that which is shared by others as just that -- a sharing of which you can take only that which will assist you as you learn to be the totality which you are.

I can see your greatness. Even as you feel of your confinement of form, I can experience the greatness which is you. I see you without the need for tool or place. I see you as the divine beings you are standing in the totality which you are. You are ten feet tall. You have no limitation beyond that which is accepted by you. You can traverse the stars, heal a nation and hold a planet. You can do this with no assistance other than the recognition of your own power as you are aligned with the Source. Accept no less.

Beloved brethren, commanders-in-space, lay aside

the use of anything external which will rob you of your own. Stand in the LIGHT of your BEINGNESS that the Source may work through you. Allow the flow of the energies from the Source to go through you to all which is about you. Stand as the save-ors of the planet to heal, uplift, and free those who are too timid to attempt that which you have achieved. I salute you.

I send forth a command-date to all ones of the Fleet to secure themselves in their locations, their stations and initiate their orders.

Ashtar, out.

Salu Salu Salu

* * * * *

Could you tell us something about these tools, for example, crystals? Are these considered good or bad, and how can they assist by having them about us?

KEILTA Greetings, dear ones of planet Earth. ...We would speak of that which are the crystals. First, let us clarify something. There is a difference between that which you call a crystal and that which is crystalline energy. Your question is of crystals. You are asking of the form.

Each crystal, if you will, has come to you because it is of the elements which have gone through a specific process, and it has come forth in a specific manner. Because it is of a specific vibration in all its energy, each crystal carries an energy. The energy is not good, it is not bad, it is an energy. You who are within your dimension are the ones who put forth the thought which programs the crystal. Crystals are tools, not crutches. If a crystal can be an assistor for you for a period, then it is fine.

In some instances you can use crystals as you will facilitate healing or balancing. However, recognize it is the thought, it is the energy which you put in it, as to how the energy of the crystal itself is used. Crystals are not good;

they are not bad. They merely contain an energy. You are the ones who direct the energy. It was never intended for a crystal to be a crutch for anyone. They are tools.

In civilizations which have been upon your plane long ago, long before I ever came to your sphere, mankind felt he could put sufficient thought into crystals, and he found that they had great power -- the thought plus the pristine energy in the crystals. And so, they were used in many ways. They were used, not always for the highest good for the consciousness at that time. There were those even in that day, if you will, who knew the power of the thought and how it could be directed and used.

Now let me speak briefly of crystalline energy, because there is a big difference. Crystalline energy is pure energy -- even as I said, your crystals are not good or bad; they merely contain an energy. You focus how it would be used. Crystalline energy is energy which is pure. It can be used multi-dimensionally. It is not limited to one or two dimensions.

Crystalline energy is the energy vibration which would go along what you would call a grid system. It is the energy which we use in many instances to power some of the ships. It is a pure energy. But you cannot tap into this crystalline energy except in a very microscopic way, until you are absolutely sure of you, how you will use it. We do not determine this, but you determine how you may and when you may. For you see, you are your best record keeper and you know how you have used certain information or knowledge in past experiences.

Within various places or points on your planet, there are crystals which have been brought to your planet from other places, if you will. Some of them have been brought into a materialization from spheres which do not contain the confinement of form. Some of them have been brought to you from other planets throughout your system or from other galactic systems. These were placed within the Earth Mother at the time she began to take on solidification.

The purpose of these are homing and communicative devices for interplanetary communication and travel. It would be the same as you building a telegraph system out into your wilderness. You would maintain a link with the ones who are there. It is the same process. The energies from these crystals can be used by ones of like vibration for recharging and for assisting them should they be in the situation of interplanetary travel or in the situation of interplanetary communication.

That which is called your National Parks or areas which have been set aside within each country for all ones of that country to enjoy, usually are areas of earth which are over such crystals. That way, no man can claim any of them, but they belong to all ones. You will note when you go into specific areas of recreation, shall we say, you come out and you feel much lighter, you have had a pleasant experience, it has been most wondrous. It is because you have released unbalances which are within you and they have been absorbed, if you will, and balanced by the crystal which is buried beneath the surface.

Usually in such places in close proximity there is that which you would call an etheric window. This etheric window is one in which we might go in and out, and you would find quite often this area will facilitate inter-dimensional communication.

MONKA (continues regarding crystalline energy) Greeting, beloveds. ...These precious, precious things you have, you have not yet fully realized their capability or their potential. Those systems which you have upon your plane which you call computer systems have been reason to destroy many crystalline fields about your planet, for the crystals have been ground, baked and molded to make small chips which might be used in your computer processes. We, too, use crystals in our -- well, shall we call them computers, if that will simplify things for you. But we do not do it in the same manner which you do.

Crystalline energy is used in most all of the areas of the Command in one way or another. Crystalline energy can be used to power space ships. It can be used as an assistor for heating. It can be used as a propulsion agent. And it can also, most vitally, be used as a communicative tool. For indeed, when I have said our "computers" -- and here, I would put this in quotes, crystals and crystalline energy is used for recording, for storing information, and for transmitting information within the Fleet. But if you will search your memory patterns, you know this, for indeed, many of you worked with this particular type of energy when you were on the planet at the close of a cycle not too many of your Earth years ago.

Crystals and crystalline energy have not come into the consciousness in their usefulness for the mass consciousness on planet Earth. There are a small number of ones who would call themselves learned, who have begun to work with crystalline energy. You will note, I have used the term "crystalline energy," rather than crystal technology or crystal energy. Just as vibratory rates of people, or Earth man, is being altered, so it is, the energy of crystals can be used, or utilized, shall I say, on more than one level. When you have an attunement and a clarity of purpose, so it is, the energy which goes through a crystal then is crystalline. It takes on a force, a power, a strength, which you have not yet experienced. But because of the attuning processes which we use, we are capable of achieving this in working with crystals.

This ability was -- shall we say, if you would like to use the past tense -- used at the time of other civilizations upon your planet. The know-how, or knowledge to do this, was freely shared with the ones who were the early inhabitants of your planet. However, because of the over zealousness of Earth mankind, it has been decided to wait until you have been a little more advanced before this knowledge and technology is shared with you. That which is being brought into being upon your planet is at a much lower vibration than the total potential holds. So I give you something to look forward to, do I not?...

When we break and fracture crystals on Earth, what does it do to the crystal and how does it affect us?

KEILTA If you can, in your minds eye, see the crystal as it weeps. For indeed, your crystals are living, they feel. They are gifts that were brought from other galaxies to planet Earth. Indeed, as each of you is aware from your readings and your studies, they have played a most vital role in your history.

Those of you that are familiar with crystals know that as you would hold one in your hand, there is a communion that is established. In some instances you will observe that a particular energy pattern of a crystal is not compatible with yours but is compatible with another. In long, distant days of your history crystals were used as homing devices. They have been used as energies that would be compared with your engines. They are used and have been used for healing, for balancing, for attuning. They can be used and have been used, to assist you in growing in your own awareness.

You, upon your planet, have been most barbaric in your attitudes toward crystals. For you have seen them as to be most crude rocks and they have been treated with no respect and dignity. Indeed, they have been forced into a state of servitude to enhance your various communication systems.

As Earth man, in his eagerness to increase his own monetary status, he has taken the quickest, most, what he would say, efficient manner, to harvest this gift. Those of you that are particularly attuned, should you enter into such an excavation area, you would indeed begin to weep. For you would feel the cries that are coming forth as these ones are crushed, are broken from their bases, are not allowed to grow to their full brightness, and are carelessly thrown about.

As you have done with that which is your natural forests, so it is that you also have done of this gift, even as you have mined for various minerals about your planet. You have had little or no regard for the gift that is being given up to you. Consequently, as you will look about, as you will become aware, these gifts are being withdrawn. Look at your forests, look at your crystalline beds, look at that which you would call your rare minerals. You have come in and you have taken with little respect. And so it is, you have entered into a phase that there is a scarcity of these.

But to return to that which are known to you as the crystal substances. These have an energy of their own. And as ones are gently removed with a state of asking, of attunement and willingness to share, the crystal is freely given up to join its energies with another for the upliftment and the use of all mankind. Until that is done -- and it is being done in very isolated instances upon your planet -- but until this is done exclusively, all of you shall feel the weeping of the crystal.

When crystals are brought to us that have been damaged, what should we do?

KEILTA As a crystal would be placed within your hand and you would feel an attunement to what this particular crystal would say to you, many of you can feel it's weeping, and you can feel that it has been plucked from its place. These ones, though it may seem questionable to you, are brought to you to be healed. For each of you has within you the ability to help heal one of these crystals, indeed, many ones.

As you would hold one, feel what it would say to you. Each of you have that which is a dwelling place. Each of you has that which is a sacred place within your dwelling place. Can this small one that has been offered up to you be placed within this sacred place that it would feel of the love, of the reverence that is within you, that it might grow and be

191

healed? And you might occasionally pick it up and hold it to your heart that it might feel your nearness and your warmth. And as you would do this, then slowly, as you would hold this one in your hand, you will feel it as it heals, until that time that it has grown in its own clarity. When it has reached that particular state then it is time that the hour it has spent with you that it might go forth that it would share its energies with another.

To summarize this, you might say that you would be healers, you would be ones that would set up infirmaries for these wounded crystals. For as they are mended -- and this is what you are doing, you are mending an energy field about and within the crystal -- then they are better able to be transformers and transmitters that would assist another one that is not as apt at assisting in their healing.

Crystals are not to be owned. Crystals are not to be possessed. But rather, there is a mutual sharing that exists. Some of you may find that there will be a particular crystal that will reside with you over long periods of time. This is done for a mutual upliftment. But know the hour will approach when that one that has served with you is to be released that it might go forth to assist another.

How important is it to wear our crystals?

MONKA ...There have been ones that would see that by wearing the quartz crystal this identifies them as one to be lifted off. Indeed, the crystal that is your passport to lift-off is that which is your heart center. Those of you that walk in truth, that walk in Light and Love of all of mankind have a heart center that is of a crystalline glow. This is the crystal that is seen by us.

Yes, you may wear the stone that is taken from your Earth as a symbol to remind yourselves of your position in your particular life pattern but the crystal that we see is the Light that comes from your heart center. You, perhaps, would call this the heart chakra. So be it. But it is the energy flow, the Light that comes forth from this that is seen by us...

What is a feeder crystal?

SARNA ...This is an energy pattern that is within a crystal that does just that, it feeds you, and it will assist you. Many of you are drawn to certain crystals as you would go into your shops, are you not?

Recognize that certain crystals carry specific energies. For as they were brought into manifestation they would be what you would call the solidification of a specific energy pattern. And there are ones that would assist you. You would pick up one and it would have a great energy for you. When that one that sits next to you would pick the same one up and say, "How pretty", and lay it down. For it is a very individual thing.

Many of you in other embodiments in other places throughout the galaxies have been one to work with solidified energy forms. And so, you would have a particular attunement or an affinity for, perhaps, one type of stone over another. But this is what you would call a feeder, it feeds. And it also will feed others, as you would have other crystals associated with it. You will find one that will give off an energy that helps to infuse the others.

If you would go into that which is your place where you would find your crystals or you would purchase them, and you would run your hands over a display of crystals, you will be able to find one that is a feeder or one that activates others. For indeed, it is keeping the energy moving within the crystal until such time as the individual comes along that has a harmonious vibration with the crystal and then it is no longer necessary. When your vibration has reached a certain attunement, then your crystal will no longer be useful for you. You will no longer need it.

Will you tell us about the crystal skulls, their origin, function and purpose please?

HATONN Greetings, dear ones of planet Earth. ...These are a result of cultures. They were introduced in a time of the Atlantean culture by ones from another star system. They have the ability to be used either as a positive or that which you would call a negative influence.

There are those that have come to the surface, shall we say, upon your planet that lack an authenticity. There are those that would carry a specific vibration with them. The original intent of these as they were brought to the planet of a distant day was one of control, and indeed, there was an energy that came forth that would be translated into that which you would call an hypnotic control. This was of a distant day.

They were introduced in a specific temple during the Atlantean period. As that which was your civilization that was known as Atlantis began to crumble, these were scattered about your planet, and they fell into hands of varied ones. Each that had these became aware of the energy that could be infused into these. And recognize, energy is not good and it is not bad. Energy is. It is what you do with it that brings about your end product. Hence, there were ones that recognized the great energies that could be stored within these crystalline structures, and they would use these for healing; they would use these to assist. They were used in many ways to foretell what would be experienced. There were others who recognized the same energy within these crystalline forms, and selected to use them in that which would be called a more devious manner. So you may take your choice.

My suggestion to any one that would become involved with these is to note what you experience. If you have an unsettled feeling, even of a photograph of these, then it is not your path to become involved. But recognize that the energy that would come of a particular one is an energy that is not in attunement for you, and it would be of no assistance.

May I add a thought for each of your considerations. At this time of the Atlantean period that I speak of, there were ones that used these for control, and indeed, you have heard of the term "to sell your soul". And so it was, there were ones that were totally controlled by the one who was the -- and I shall not use the word "owner", but who was the keeper of the skull. And so it was, they were used as a great power tool. Be aware of this, and in all ways recognize of your own discernment capabilities and allow no thing to become your master.

What is the role of music in raising our vibratory rate?

BEATRIX Greeting, beloveds. ...That which you call music is a series of energies at a specific vibration. You know there is music you like and there is music you do not like. You know there is some music which makes you want to cry and there is some music which makes you feel very uplifted. And there is some of it that it would be as it was very healing and soothing to you. You would find there are certain selections that are old friends, are they not? But take music one step and see it as tone. Music is the expression of tone within your dimension. Tones are specific vibrations which go forth which can produce color; they can be communicative; they can be tuning.

And so, in working with music, what you are doing is you are taking specific vibrations within your dimension. And because they are balancing, because they are comforting, because they are not unbalancing to another one, they will assist the other one to be in a relaxed state, if you will, of receptivity. And the focus is one of a balancing; it is one of an uplifting nature, so that the individual may then go into that which is the realm of tone. And that is the role of music. It is to be enjoyed, it is to be danced, it is to be sung, it is to be used in all expressions. But you will note you are in a period

-- and you have been in period since approximately, I would say, the last half of your century -- in which you have had a great intense bombardment of sound. I did not say "music" -- I said "sound." And it would be as if it was just hitting at you, hmm? This is an attempt to lock you within your own vibrational pattern and to limit your own growth.

If you have the instruments, you will find the technology is available in which there are various subliminal messages which go into this "thing", even as you have with your machines. There are subliminal messages that program. And at first you do not realize this. And then you find, for those of you who have a sensitivity, you can listen to this and you'll find something of an irritation, and you generally are irritated all over. And it is such an irritation, it would be as if you can feel prickly feelings all over you. It is your vibration in conflict with the subliminal vibration which is coming forth.

Can you tell us more about music and its power to heal and balance?

BEATRIX Think if you will of light, that which you know is light. Think of your colors of the spectrum and see them dance. Though many of you do not have the particular gift at this time, as you strike a musical note an energy vibration goes forth. This energy produces sound. It produces color. It produces vibration. These are interwoven and intermingled.

Recognizing that each of you are a condensation in form of energy, it is highly probable that the energy within your being would react to music, to color, to the vibration that each puts forth. And as your instruments of your orchestras are tuned to absolute pitch, it is possible, it is probable that the earthly vehicle, instrument, may also be tuned to absolute pitch in sound and in color that it might vibrate at a frequency which is of the absolute.

Now in the upcoming days, as Earth changes its rotational pattern, and that era which you have termed the New Age comes forth, ones will be readily available to assist in helping to attune the instruments that you call your physical beings. This is a direct form of healing that has been used on the other planets for eons. And at one time it was the accepted method of healing on Earth; however, as man -- and here I speak of Earth man -- as he has digressed from his original route, he has lost the ability to tune this instrument.

What about such things as medications?

EMARTUS Greetings and salutations. ...In the not too distant day you will find your chemical potions given by the ones who are called healers, your physicians, will be of no use or service to you.

You will find your physical beings respond to natural balancing much more rapidly and more comfortably. For when one is in a state they require healing, merely you are bringing balance to unbalance, are you not? And you are balancing yourself. So as facilitators, you will allow energy to flow to one who is not in balance to assist them to bring balance to themselves.

However, you who are in the form of your dimensional limitation find you are looking at your fluid intake, you are looking at the foods you put in your being, you are looking at water. Do you know that substance? Many of you run from it. It can be used internally, not just to bathe in. Bathing is another tool to assist in bringing your own being into balancing.

Allowing the physical vehicle to rest, challenging your minds, allowing expression of your emotions -- these are all tools for you to use. As you do this and you recognize this, so it is you come into a greater balance and the greater balance then allows a purer flow through you, for you have not muddied it, shall we say.

Is Hydrogen Peroxide helpful in oxygenating the body?

EMARTUS ...For some yes, for others no. If you would desire to know if it is the answer for you then you would try it. There is no one thing which is good for all ones. Many products have come forth which have been given as a tool. However, your stamp of approval for a particular substance has been, "It will cure everything", and this is not accurate. For each vehicle is different. Each soul pattern is different. And each intent is different. So it is one must find what is right, what is best for them.

You have that which is muscle testing, do you not? You have that which is the use of a pendulum, do you not? See what is right for you. If you do not trust that innate knowing that is within you, then use one of these techniques for a confirmation.

And I will add a part here... Do you know you have within you, if you will use your own power, the ability to balance out anything and everything. All you can do, all you must do is know you can do this. You can hold a glass of water, of juice, of whatever you would desire, or a piece of fruit or anything and you would say, "From the Totality that I Am, I would infuse this, 'whatever it is', that I might receive only that which is for my highest good, all else going forth to be transmuted into its original perfection." And then you may do your muscle testing, your pendulum, to see if there has been a molecular change. And indeed you will find that there has been. It is a simple thing to do. But there is one catch to this. You must eat or drink all of that which you have zapped.

The actual saying is not of a great consequence. What is of the consequence is what is within you, knowing you have the power to balance out within this, whatever it is for your highest good -- knowing that within yourself, you command it from the Lord God of your Totality. And know you are capable of doing this. And then you may do your pendulum or your muscle testing or whatever it is. And I would strongly urge each of you before you place your head upon the pillow this night to try this, to confirm to yourself that you can do it. It is important that you recognize this.

So to return to your original question, it is a very individual thing. And anyone who would enter into your plane and say to you, "Here is the potion, this is the answer for everything," you look at them and you smile and you say "thank you" and in your wisdom you know that they have not walked their path as long as you have walked yours.

What about herbs?

EMARTUS Herbs -- they are natural gifts that can assist in your balancing if they are used with discernment. May I underscore <u>discernment</u>. For there are those upon the planet that would become so involved with particular modes of doing things that they would become a little over zealous, especially with that which are the herbs for they are delicate and they will assist in the delicate balancing, cleansing, and attunement of form.

Is Super Blue Green Algae a good food for humanity at this time? Would it enhance the raising of our vibration and bring us into balance?

EMARTUS ...You ask of this potion which has become quite in vogue upon your plane. In the days that are before you, there shall be more and more potions that come to your awareness and each one will be branded as the absolute for you, that it will bring you into whatever you need. And if you are short, it will make you tall. If you are tall it will make you short.

First, examine each of you why you would take these things. Why do you put these potions within your form? It is to bring a balance, is it not? Now you can desire balance for two reasons. One reason can be in order to have a temple which is the fit dwelling place for the spirit. The other can be that which is, "I won't let go of what I've got, and I would desire to hold on to this form through all eternity because there is a thought in the back of my mind that though I proclaim to say I am eternal, I don't really know if I am or not." So examine the motive, why you would take this. Then sit down with a sampling of whatever it is you would take, hold it in your hand, and ask your form, "Do you need this? Is this what you need?" And then to sound rather brusk, I would suggest you be quiet and listen to see what your form tells you.

You cannot be expressed deity as long as you take all of the advice that others would give you for you must be the deciding factor for you. There would be those that would say to you, if you eat of a certain fruit three times a day that you would have a great wisdom. And there are those of you on your plane who would eat of this fruit and you would find your I.Q. has not improved one bit, hmm?

There are those who would be called charlatans. Do you know this word? And there is that which is called "hoax". Do you know that word? They shall become quite rampant. As your cycle comes to a close, this whole activity shall accelerate. But may I suggest to you that whatever it is you feel you would want to put within your form, you ask it, you wait to see what you feel, what your form tells you, and then you simply run your hand over it and ask that it be for your highest good.

We have technology which will magnify the delta-theta frequencies of the brain. Can this help us in inter-communication?

JOKHYM   Salutations, my brothers and sisters of planet Earth. ...The key to what you said, my brother, is, "We have technology which will..." With that technology, you can control the thinking process -- not thought, but the thinking process. Recognize your brain is but a receiver. You could say it is a filing system, so to speak. But your mind goes out far beyond your physical understanding, and it interacts with the energy vibrations beyond the brain. The brain merely stores this information. By altering the electrical frequency of the brain, you alter the -- let me choose my thought carefully -- you alter the level of receptivity and reclamation which can be done within that which is the form, or the organ which you call the brain.

The inter-dimensional communication which would come about in such a manner is limiting and myopic, because it does not include the totality of balancing the entity who is involved in the experience. But rather, it is only the experience of alteration of frequency. It is not the alteration of the frequency for the totality which is an alteration in the whole vibrational pattern. It is only an alteration in the brain frequencies. And you will at best receive a limited communication.

It has also been used in the past, and it is found it is a very expeditious way to control mankind. Indeed, the whole thinking process can be altered to the point there is no thinking, per se; no mental capacity -- just the electrical action of the brain. The interaction or the other half of the formula, if you will, is completely omitted.

Technology is a wonderful tool, and it is through your technology you learn many things which you can do on your own. You can do the same thing without the alteration, the external stimuli and alteration within the frequency pattern of the brain. In some instances where this is being done you are not actually reaching an inter-dimensional communication, but you are tapping into memories of previous experiences, is what you are doing, and you are using this as a recall system; though to the one who is hearing this for the first time it is not a recall, but it would appear as a new experience.

If I were upon your plane and I had opportunity to experience this, I would select to go the other way because it does not take into account the totality which I Am, and it does not take into account my experiences of my divinity and what I am led for or how I am led, and what my primary lead force is. But it is tapping into that which is not explained, and that is the way it is presented...

The extra low frequency is being used in this same manner, and again, it is a control situation. So it is not that which can be a lasting situation. It is an interim.

...Now there have been, as you are aware, machines if you will -- transmitters and receivers -- which have been built upon your plane which have allowed for inter-dimensional communication. Really it has. However, the communication has not been an extended one -- extended over much of a lifetime, for instance -- but it has been for a segment of years. Specific information has been brought forth, and then your governments have not been comfortable with the situation. So individuals have been removed, or machines -- shall we say, transmitters and receivers -- have been destroyed. At best these machines have only been a verification of the existence beyond your dimension. You have that communicative ability within each of you...

How better can the Violet Flame be used?

MONKA ...Before I would speak, I would establish specific parameters for my reply, for I do not speak as one that is an authority on the transmuting flame. To stir your recollection, about the time of the close of your Atlantean cycle the transmuting flame was used by all. It was placed within the temples, and all that was not of balance, of harmony was freely given over to the Flame which absorbed it, and returned it in its elemental form. Unfortunately, at that particular stage of evolution there were those that were known as the temple priests who chose to limit the use of this Flame to only that which they considered as appropriate. In your current jargon, they set themselves up as a go-between, and thus the use of the Flame was greatly reduced. There were those that used it not in truth, but used it for their own personal gain. There were even ones that went so far as to charge a fee for allowing one to place anything within the Flame. And so the Flame was withdrawn from man's consciousness.

The beloved master known to you as St. Germain has gone before the Council, the Hierarchial Board and asked that this again be restored to the consciousness of man, that man in this close of his cycle might have the ability to transmute his soul's unbalances as well as those that are with him now. This has been done at great sacrifice in an attempt to assist man in raising his own conscious awareness into a higher developmental state. So the Flame has been freed that man, Earth man, might call upon this freely that he might place his unbalances, his disharmonies in this flame to be transmuted into that which are the primordial elements that are of the Oneness.

There are several ways that have been given to various ones upon your planet to call forth this flame. The primary objective is to consciously and knowingly place your unbalances within it that they might have opportunity to be transmuted.

Here I will offer another thought for your consideration. As you have removed your unbalances, you have left open areas within yourselves. May I suggest to you that you would fill these with the White Light, with the Christ Light, which ever term is comfortable for you to use, that no additional unbalances might creep in, but rather that you are filled with the White Light.

May I suggest to each of you, that you consciously look at your activities and to look at that which brings about an unbalance for you, and when this comes to your awareness, stop, offer this unbalance to the Flame that it might be transmuted. This shall assist each of you in your own evolution as well as assisting mankind in its upliftment.

Please explain the use of decreeing?

SARNA If you will trace the steps of that which is Earth mankind, you will find that you have gone through various growth processes. Each served a purpose of that particular stage of growth. Mantras, decrees, have a place if they are used as tools to assist one to attain a higher consciousness. But anything, be they crystals, be they a favorite brooch, a chair, or a rock, when they become the object of a concentration then the whole meaning has been lost, for each is but a tool to assist in a higher consciousness.

And one might say, "I would say this mantra ten times o'er", and another would say that they must follow a specific ritual and they must sit in a certain manner. That is fine if this assists them to attain a higher consciousness. But if it so binds them that they cannot attain the consciousness without the tool, then the tool has become the master, and that was not the intent of the tool.

There is no one that is seen as the energy pattern upon my screen (within the audience) that has need for specific mantras, for specific thoughts, for specific rituals that they have need to follow, for each has within them the knowledge of the Christ consciousness, that they are of the Totality of all creation, and that they have to have no gimmicks, no rituals to follow in order to be able to attune to that which is the Divinity. This is the thought that is projected for all ones, and this is the desire that all ones would hold this thought.

Is there any value in going into past lives to understand why we might have fears about certain things now?

ATHENA Greetings in the Light of the Source to each of you.

...In individual cases it can be advantageous to review past experiences to determine the reason for the fear pattern. However, at this point in your cycle, I would urge that those of you do not dwell upon past experiences, but rather go forward and greet and meet new ones.

Some of you have gone through a phase of, "I was so-and-so". This has done no appreciable good to assist you in your evolution. In the event that one of you -- and here, again may I stress this is an individual situation -- experiences an undue fear concerning a specific situation then it would be best to go back, back until such time as the reason for this fear is brought to your conscious awareness that you might deal with this to go on. This is the one situation that I might suggest that it would be beneficial to review past life experiences.

If you choose to delve into that which is your history, may I suggest to you that you would ask that only that be revealed which would assist you this day, which would assist you to go forth to manifest your own perfection.

Can semiconscious trance channelling of our own over-soul be a way to enhance our own learning? Is this process to flourish in others soon?

HATONN No! No! No! No! No! Have I made myself clear? You of Earth love gimmicks, and you would greatly desire shortcuts as you would call them. Or you would very muchly like to have a small book that would be a cram book instead of taking the whole course. Is this not true, my dear ones? Yes, you know this is true.

Quiet contemplation, conscious awareness, study, the melding of facts and knowing within your being is your key to your greater wisdom. There are no shortcuts. There are no crash courses that are given.

Ones would desire to speak with their higher self. Do

so. You are quite capable of this with your eyes open, your consciousness seated firmly between your shoulders, and your voice in a normal tone. I do not, and I have not recommended that altered states of consciousness be experienced unless one is individually guided to this method. Here again, may I underline the word, <u>individually</u>. And in such instances they know who they are. But recognize that which you desire to know, you are quite capable of knowing as you sit in the comfort of your chair. There is no need to attempt altered states of consciousness to see what would happen. For this is merely playing at games with tools you are not familiar with that might be more harmful than they would create good for you. And so as I have said, no, no, no!...

* * * * *

My dear compatriots, as we close our portion of the discussion so do we also close this volume. It is our desire for you to take with you thoughts which might assist to answer questions, or in some instances to cause new ones for you. Be challenged. Be all you can be. No tool can do that for you, only you can.

In this series of classes, we have attempted to share thoughts related to you and your own process. Many of you have struggled and are struggling with mighty loads. As you release them so it is, you too shall become Lighter and Lighter until you recognize you are the crystalline meeting place, the point of reception and dissemination for your own growth. You are the assistor of others as you better understand your own life experience. Walk in peace.

Sarna, out.

Publications By

Portals of Light, Inc.

Talks With The Masters: Theoaphylos

Talks With The Masters: El Morya

Talks With The Masters: Serapis Bey

Letters From Home: Vol. I

Letters From Home: Vol. II

Letters From Home: Vol. III

Letters From Home: Vol. IV

Conclave: Meeting Of The Ones

Conclave: 2nd Meeting

Conclave: 3rd Meeting

Conclave: 4th Meeting

Hello, I'm Tobias. Can I Come Talk To You?